Start & Run a Pet Business

Heather Mueller
BSW, RSW

Self-Counsel Press
(a division of)
International Self-Counsel Press Ltd.
USA   Canada

Copyright©2011 by International Self-Counsel Press Ltd.

All rights reserved.

No part of this book may be reproduced or transmitted in any form by any means — graphic, electronic, or mechanical — without permission in writing from the publisher, except by a reviewer who may quote brief passages in a review.

Self-Counsel Press acknowledges the financial support of the Government of Canada through the Canada Book Fund (CBF) for our publishing activities.

Printed in Canada.

First edition: 2011

Library and Archives Canada Cataloguing in Publication

Mueller, Heather, 1979–
    Start & run a pet business / Heather Mueller.

ISBN 978-1-77040-092-4

    1. Pet industry — Management. 2. Pet industry — Vocational guidance. 3. New business enterprises — Management. I. Title. II. Title: Start and run a pet business.

SF414.7.M84 2011   636.088'70681   C2011-904548-6

Self-Counsel Press
(a division of)
International Self-Counsel Press Ltd.

Bellingham, WA   North Vancouver, BC
USA   Canada

Contents

Notice to Readers

Laws are constantly changing. Every effort is made to keep this publication as current as possible. However, the author, the publisher, and the vendor of this book make no representations or warranties regarding the outcome or the use to which the information in this book is put and are not assuming any liability for any claims, losses, or damages arising out of the use of this book. The reader should not rely on the author or the publisher of this book for any professional advice. Please be sure that you have the most recent edition.

Note: The fees quoted in this book are correct at the date of publication. However, fees are subject to change without notice. For current fees, please check with the court registry or appropriate government office nearest you.

Prices, commissions, fees, and other costs mentioned in the text or shown in samples in this book probably do not reflect real costs where you live. Inflation and other factors, including geography, can cause the costs you might encounter to be much higher or even much lower than those we show. The dollar amounts shown are simply intended as representative examples.

Acknowledgements

I would like to thank Self-Counsel Press for making this book possible. Thanks to my wonderful editor, Tanya Lee Howe, for all of her assistance with this project from start to finish.

A special thank you to my husband, Kurt, for all of his love, support, and encouragement.

Last but never least, thank you to all the animals I have had the privilege to know. They have taught me many lessons, and gave me the experience I needed to write this book.

I dedicate this book to my mother, Cindy Orcutt, whose unconditional love of animals will always be my inspiration.

Introduction

It has been my privilege over the past eight years to do what I love most each and every day. The experiences I have gained in that time have been both emotionally and physically rewarding. My experiences clearly affirm I have chosen the best career path I could have for myself by working with animals. Although, I cannot take all the credit, as I did come by the choice honestly; coming from a family of ranchers and being raised in a small town in Alberta, Canada, provided endless opportunities to be around a variety of animals.

I started my work with animals because of an inherent love for all creatures. Throughout the years I have been very fortunate to work with animals in many different capacities, such as animal rescue, animal-assisted therapy, and animal homeopathic practitioner.

While completing my Bachelor of Social Work degree, I learned of an innovative therapy technique called animal-assisted therapy. The primary goal of this therapy was to utilize the human-animal bond to promote trust and respect in client-therapist relations. The more I researched this innovative concept, the more excited I became. Finally a way to meld animals with my chosen profession; in Canada, 80 percent of therapists or counselors are registered social workers.

I was elated because I had found the ultimate career. The only problem was that no agency or organization had implemented anything like this in my city at that time. This surprised me greatly, as there was strong support for various animal businesses and services in the area. The bulk of my research indicated that the practice models for animal-assisted therapies support the idea that human-animal interactions can produce positive psychological and physiological benefits in both humans and animals. This theory is based on thousands of years of human anecdotal evidence. At the time the Chimo Project had also just released groundbreaking, solid empirical evidence supporting this idea.

I did the only thing I could think of and created Pets for Health Sake, Animal-Assisted Therapies Services. My rationale was simple: If there were no services like this then I would ensure that there would be. With the support of my employers at the time, we established a joint program, at first, between the Schizophrenia Society (Lethbridge and area chapter) and the Canadian Mental Health Association (Lethbridge/Alberta South Region). Because of their trust in my professional abilities to pioneer this concept within our city, and their own experiences of the healing power of animals, I was able to create a flexible program that delved into all aspects of human-animal interaction therapies. The program's mission statement was clear: "To provide individuals the opportunity to interact with animals and receive the benefits thereof."

I have had the pleasure of working with rabbits, cats, bearded dragons, and dogs in a variety of different ways; facilitating everything from literacy to young offender programs. Focusing on each animal's individual abilities and strengths I sought to create strategies that would reflect the unique benefits of each animal for humans.

During that time I also became involved with the Lethbridge & District Humane Society, first as an office volunteer then as Vice President of the Board of Directors and eventually President. President was a title I held proudly through two consecutive two-year terms. By working with the Humane Society animals and becoming aware of their varying ailments, I became interested in different options for treating the animals with which I was in contact. I found many of the Western approaches to animal medicine seemed to lack a cure for progressive chronic symptoms. This in turn led to years of me researching various natural and Eastern modalities and methods.

While completing my certification as an Animal Homeopathic Practitioner I offered my services to the community through Tail Blazers (Lethbridge), Inc. With emerging companies such as Healthy Spot in Santa Monica, California, and Tail Blazers Inc., originating from Calgary, Alberta, I was able to expand on the concept of a retail-health-food store for pets catering to all aspects of the whole being of the animal, from nutrition to health care. With my background and certification, and the support of Tail Blazers' Lethbridge owner, Tammy Luchansky, the Lethbridge franchise was the first of the Tail Blazers stores to be able to offer this type of a business combination.

My focus has always been to improve the pet industry, no matter on which side of it I became involved. Throughout the past eight years I have chosen to introduce emerging trends and innovative ideas to my community while working with animals.

As the pet industry continues to expand at an accelerating and unprecedented rate, there are endless possibilities when it comes to creating a successful pet business. With a little ingenuity and a solid business plan the sky is truly the limit for this industry.

What I have learned from my experiences working with animals has been instrumental in my continued personal and professional successes. It is my hope in writing this book that you will also be able to create a successful and ethical venture that expresses your love of animals.

Chapter 1

The Different Types of Pet Businesses

The first thing you must ask yourself is: Why do you want to start a pet business? Is it because of your love for animals or solely for the hope of creating a profitable venture? Will you attempt to fill a gap in the industry or create a niche market?

As with any business you must have a clear and concise objective as to the type of business you want to start, and what benefits that business will provide to your clients and community. Defining your motives in the beginning will give you and potential investors an idea of the future profitability of your business. When looking at the overall consumer activity in the pet industry, an increasingly upward trend has developed in the last decade, taking what used to be a conservative multimillion-dollar industry, into a staggering multibillion-dollar industry.

Once you've decided what your particular focus is you can start focusing on other aspects such as location, regulations, population (statistics), business plan, and future expansion.

I have broken down the overview of various business opportunities into sections in this chapter, rather than into individual businesses. Frankly, there are just too many viable business options to go into too much detail on all of them. The sections that follow cover businesses that can be described as services, health care, retail, or nonprofit or volunteer.

1. Service

Businesses that fall under the service category in the pet industry can included but are certainly not limited to the following:

- Pet finder
- Agility training
- Obedience training
- Pet sitting
- Pet grooming
- Pet visitation programs
- Animal-assisted therapy

3

- Pet memorial services
- Dog-walking
- Doggy daycares or kennels

Most of these types of services require that the providers have some form of acceptable certification within their area. Depending on which type of pet service you wish to provide, certifications in the service industry can be obtained through courses that take a few weekends or evenings to a couple of years in college.

Before you sign up for courses, research any institution or organization to make sure that it is recognized by your state or province. Pay special attention to who or what within the pet industry recognizes these certifications. Aside from some specialized services, it is wise to pick a course that is nationally recognized, versus just locally recognized. State, provincial, and federal mandates regarding the type of certification required to offer certain services, such as training or grooming, will differ depending on your location. Be aware of what your municipality expects when you obtain your business license. For example, should you decide to open a doggy daycare in the same location as a pizzeria, some municipalities will not allow a food service combined with an animal-based business. Depending on the region in which your business will be located, and what services you wish to provide, your facility may need to be approved by your local health authority. Be apprised of local health requirements and municipal bylaws regarding types of services *before* you create your business plan.

It is also advisable to research health and safety standards in your area. You should strive to meet or exceed the current standards. Not only does this help to establish credibility of your new business, it also keeps you ahead of the game. If you choose to do less than what is expected of you in an effort to curb start-up costs, it could result in failure or having to spend time or money to catch up to current standards.

When opening a service-based business, an easy to clean location is a must (see Chapter 4 for more information about picking a location). Look at properties that have concrete or vinyl flooring or plan for this as part of your renovation costs in your business plan. Note that a pet-service business can range anywhere from $10,000 to $50,000 (USD or CAD) on average in start-up costs.

When providing services for animals you must have a contingency plan in place in case the unforeseen should occur. Depending on your specialty and training, most associations will already have guidelines or suggestions for contingency plans. Be sure to research these so you are educated as to what is considered the best practices model for your given venue. You should also create a more specific version of your contingency plan, which includes what is required of you by any association you may belong to as well as points specific to your particular venue.

Consider every worst-case scenario you can and then write a policy and procedure manual for how you would handle each situation. This should be done on some level for all types of pet businesses. Even in retail you and your employees should know how to handle an upset customer before you ever have to deal with one in person.

Based on the one-stop-shop approach, service providers are catering to the business of today's consumers and benefiting from the extra revenues. You will have to decide if providing one service or many services is what you want to do and whether you will incorporate it at the beginning, in future expansions, or not at all. Some considerations will include hiring support staff, or perhaps a receptionist (see Chapter 7 for more on hiring staff).

2. Health Care

Pet businesses that fall under the health-care category include, but are not limited to the following:

- Veterinary clinics and hospitals
- Rehabilitation therapy centers
- Animal communicators
- Animal therapists
- Homeopathic practitioners

When looking at health-care pet businesses the first thing you should be aware of are the training requirements, as most opportunities in these fields will require a higher level of education or training. For example veterinarians, chiropractors, physiotherapists, veterinarian technologists, massage therapists, and acupuncturists all need higher education.

This is not to say you could not start a business in these fields without specific training. Typically, owners of these types of businesses perform the services themselves, rather than hire those with the required skill set. This leads to owners that have a sound knowledge base of their business, and the services they provide. This also minimizes the stress of dealing with employees with a higher level of training than yourself as it is difficult to critique their performance if you really have no understanding of their duties or requirements. Be realistic in your endeavors. After all, seldom do you see a person who can't boil water opening a restaurant!

Within the service industry, health-care services and providers will be regulated differently state to state, and province to province. Depending on the type of health-care service you will provide, the necessary training can take anywhere from six months to eight years, depending on your state or provincial requirements. Your local health authority will definitely be involved in the start-up process. Get to know the officials you will have to deal with on a regular basis through start-up and the duration of your business. It is far easier to work with someone you are familiar with and, depending on how long you own your business, you may work with a specific person continually.

Most start-up costs for businesses in the health-care field will cost $30,000 to $150,000 (USD or CAD). This will include things such as leasing or a down payment on a location, advertising, renovations, and marketing. This does not include the cost of your education or certification.

3. Retail

Retail pet businesses include, but are not limited to, the following:

🐾 Stores (e.g., food, clothing, toys, herbal and natural supplements)

🐾 Boutique stores

🐾 Online stores

When choosing a business in the pet-retail industry you have considerable options with little-to-no need for specialized training or certifications. When reviewing different pet-retail options, consider the following questions:

🐾 Do you have any moral or ethical standards for the companies from which you choose to purchase products?

- What is your budget for purchasing products?
- Will you be creating the products yourself? If so, what are your business standards and practices?
- Are you attempting to serve a niche market or a general population?

When you have answered these questions, you then need to consider what method you will use for your retail-pet operation. There are generally two standardized methods of operating a retail business: online or storefront. Whichever you choose should be based on target market, best method for product delivery, and location of your business.

3.1 Online retail

Online pet boutiques are a modern trend that is beginning to dominate the industry. These businesses are versatile, convenient, and trendy, which make them a popular choice for many would-be business owners. Online businesses are also typically less expensive to run in terms of overhead costs, start-up costs, and the nonexistence of the legal liability of signing a rental lease or purchasing a building associated with storefront businesses.

Overhead costs for online businesses range from $1,200 to $20,000 (USD or CAD). Some websites claim to be able to help you start an online business for less than $1,000, but there are always conditions, so do your research. Check references, look up the business on the Better Business Bureau website, and ask for recommendations of others as you don't want to have to pay for any aspect of your new pet business twice.

Start-up costs associated with this type of business can include ordering the product you wish to sell, setting up an online payment system, computer, high-speed Internet connection and modem, business license, specialized packaging for your products, and office supplies.

Online retail businesses are a popular option for entrepreneurs with low funds or for those who wish to avoid high risks. What's more, online retail is a great business to run as a home-based or part-time entrepreneur because it offers flexibility on the time commitment needed. It can be a fantastic outlet for your creative talent or hobby. It is also a great platform to target national and international markets right from the start.

3.2 Storefront

Storefront businesses appeal to the consumer on two basic levels. The first is that products are tactile; people generally like to touch and inspect items they are interested in purchasing. The second is impulsiveness; some people find it more appealing to buy and take home the product right then and there instead of waiting seven to ten business days to enjoy their purchase.

When opening a storefront pet-retail business, your location is what your customers will associate your product with. In many ways it will be the face of your business. Successful storefront pet-retail businesses are generally bright, clean, and open, allowing customers, two-legged and four-legged alike, easy access to products and merchandise.

As with any business, create your displays to be fun and educational. This not only attracts the customer's eye, but also reduces time-consuming questions regarding product information.

Costs associated with start-up of a retail business can range from $10,000 to $100,000 (USD or CAD), depending on your target market. Such factors can include location, overhead, equipment, wholesale prices of products and merchandise, renovations, employees, and marketing.

4. Nonprofit and Volunteer Work

Those wanting to create a nonprofit- or volunteer-based venture are not in it for the income. Nonprofit usually means low wages (if any wages at all), especially when dealing in the realm of pets. Many nonprofit or volunteer businesses are very successful, but success is not often based on economic gain. The following services fall into the volunteer or nonprofit sector of the pet business:

- Shelters
- Rescue groups
- Search and rescue
- Assistance groups (e.g., Blankets for a Cause)
- Pet visitation services

Becoming a volunteer at a local animal rescue association is a great way to network with potential supporters of your new business. It is also a valuable way to gain knowledge of working with various types of animals.

Volunteer and rescue groups are mostly created as nonprofit organizations. However, some are not operated as businesses or have business subsidiaries to help fund their efforts. Different business practices and legal requirements apply and these will vary from one jurisdiction to the next.

For many people, the reason behind creating a nonprofit organization is that a gap in services needs to be filled, rather than the motivation to create a lucrative business. It has been my experience that although very rewarding, those who create nonprofit or volunteer pet businesses are not doing so to make money. It is their passion and love for animals that drives them.

Be aware of all local and state or provincial laws pertaining to the creation of a nonprofit organization. The application process can be tedious. However, depending on your location, there are government services in place to provide assistance with the application process. Check with your local government office for more information.

Be aware that most current state and provincial laws require that in order to be a registered nonprofit organization there must be direction by an appointed board. Therefore, you may create the organization and be its founder, but you may have to defer delegation to your appointed board. Note that in Canada it is illegal to be a paid employee while sitting on the board of a nonprofit organization.

One of the main reasons in creating a nonprofit organization is the tax incentives or reductions that are offered due to low profits (if any). Grants are also more readily available to those in the nonprofit sector. Some choose this method as a way to fill the gap without having to rely on personal funding for the endeavor. There is also the ability to fundraise for your cause. Events such as dog jogs, benefit concerts, and silent dinners and auctions can be a multifunctional way to generate revenue while networking within your community. Depending on the event, you could also have a lot of fun!

Chapter 2

Prepare Your Business Plan

Preparing a business plan will help you learn more about your industry, develop new and innovative ideas, and identify the weaknesses and strengths in your business. In the United States and Canada, both the federal and state or provincial governments offer excellent business plan templates, advice, and resources for no charge. The Internet has endless information on writing business plans and many templates as well.

Your business plan will allow you to plan for the future of your pet business and identify potential problems that can and will arise. The business plan will also be used to attract investors, banks, government small-business programs, and other financial institutions for the purpose of obtaining financing.

The business plan is a comprehensive document that is created to describe the direction and projected outcome of your business. You should understand your plan inside and out and be able to clearly articulate why the business will succeed and how it is going to eventually achieve this success.

If you require outside funding, the investor should be able to read the plan and understand right from the start what the business entails and what the financial return will be. You must support any claims and projections that you have made regarding the business by providing examples and details of your experience in the market as well as including financial details. Unrealistic financial projections will more than likely lose investors' interest.

A typical business plan may consist of about 20 pages although some business plans can be 100 pages or more, depending on the plan and the nature of the business. For a pet business about 15 to 30 pages will be enough.

You might want to consider hiring outside consultants to write your business plan if you are having trouble preparing it properly for investors. However, it is always best for you to be the author of your own plan, even if you decide to bring in outside help to review and refine it. This way you will know your business intimately. Often, entrepreneurs do not take the time, nor do they feel a business plan is necessary for their businesses to succeed. This could not be further from the truth especially when building a business from the ground up.

A business plan allows you to be aware of potential problems, identify growth opportunities, and highlight possible funding opportunities. A business plan should be used as a flexible guideline for the business rather than a strict policy to be adhered to and never wavered from.

Entrepreneurial training is becoming a significant component of many learning institutions in response to the escalating numbers of business start-ups in North America. Look into community college entrepreneur programs in your area for help starting up your business and putting together your plan.

1. What Goes into a Business Plan?

It is critical that you know what you are doing before you write a business plan. It is often said that more than 70 percent of new businesses fail after the second year. As an owner of a business, knowing what to do with it is the key to being in the 30 percent of businesses that do succeed after two years. Creating a well-executed business plan will enhance the odds that your business will be one of the ones to succeed.

The following sections discuss the components of what should go into your business plan.

1.1 Executive summary

Although it leads off the business plan, the executive summary should be written last. That way, you can pull information from the rest of the report, and make certain there are no inconsistencies.

The executive summary is the introduction to a formal business plan. It summarizes the business proposition, key financial projections, where the business stands at present, and the elements that are critical for success. While you may be tempted to rush through this part, remember this is the first thing a potential investor will read. If your executive summary doesn't grab his or her attention, then he or she probably won't bother reading the rest of your plan.

A good executive summary ranges from half a page to two pages; anything longer and you risk losing your reader's attention or appearing unfocused. A safe bet is to keep it to one page or less.

1.2 Mission statement

A mission statement is a sentence or short paragraph describing a company's function, target markets, and competitive advantages. It summarizes your business goals and philosophies.

The mission statement should define who your primary customers are, identify the service or product you will offer, and describe the area in which you will operate.

Try creating one by writing down in one sentence the purpose of your business; remember this is not a slogan so it does not have to be catchy, just accurate and precise. The mission statement will show your employees and clients what your business is all about. If you are unclear about what you plan to offer, then your employees and clients will be too.

1.3 History and background

The history and background section should be about half a page to a couple of pages long. You will want to give investors or the bank a good idea of who you are and why you will succeed in this endeavor. Information to include in this section includes:

* The origin of the idea for the business
* Your education level
* Other businesses you have worked for that are relevant to the pet industry
* Your area of expertise in the industry
* Any relevant associations, clubs, or societies to which you belong
* Your areas of strength and weakness and how you plan to offset your weaknesses
* Your technical skills

1.4 Description of your business

This is where you offer more detail about the type of business you want to open, who the customers will be, and what your business's competitive advantage is.

The business description usually begins with a short description of the industry. When describing the industry, discuss the present outlook as well as future possibilities. You should provide information on all the various markets within the industry, including any new products or developments that will benefit or adversely affect your business.

Base all of your observations on reliable data and be sure to cite or footnote sources of information. This is important if you're seeking funding because the investor or financial institution will want to know just how dependable your information is, and won't risk money on assumptions or guesses. From here, you'll move on to a brief description of your financial outlook. This part should mention the expected costs of starting up as well as your bottom-line financial projections for the short and long term.

1.5 Company values

In essence, your company values are what make customers choose your business instead of your competition. Customers will compare the value of your pet business against that of your competitors when deciding where to take their business.

Try to make this section of your business plan short and precise. Your company's values explain why customers should buy from you. If you can't sum it up in 15 words or less, chances are you won't be able to execute it.

You should target the clients you want with precision and unique solutions. This is about your customer, not you, so know your customer. Your company's values should discuss only what is applicable to your clients and the value you can bring to them. Value comes in numerous forms such as money, time, convenience, and superior products.

1.6 Operations and employees

Any pet business relies on an operational plan to show how the service or product will be delivered to the client. The operations and employees part of the business plan also shows which person is in charge of what activities within the business.

You need to show the ownership of the business in terms of the partners' individual shares and contributions to the business, as well as identify the responsibilities of management. You will need to list the "decision makers" and the "action takers" and their places in the business structure.

This section will also outline the number of employees you intend to hire, how you will manage them, and your estimated personnel costs. Summarize important employee regulations and policies. Details and examples of such policies may be included in the appendixes of the business plan.

An accurate projection of the demand for your product is paramount to a successful operational strategy. The more focused your business concept is, the greater the likelihood that you'll attract investors and customers.

1.6a Location and facilities

Describe the site of your business, the facilities that are presently in place, the facility (leasehold) improvements required and/or desired, and the features that make this an attractive site for your venture. If applicable, attach sketches and drawings of the layout and plans for the site. Be sure to include financial costs and time frames for renovations or leasehold improvements.

1.6b Equipment

Describe the necessary office, mechanical, operational, and transportation equipment that is required to run the business. Make a note if any of the equipment is already owned or needs to be acquired. If it is to be acquired, state whether it will be leased or purchased, and the costs involved in doing so.

1.7 Market research

In the market research section of your business plan you will describe your target market. This includes demographic profiles, the geographic location, economic trends, and projections for the growth or decline of the market.

Research this and include a market-share analysis which shows how your business will affect the market and how much of that market you can reasonably capture. Indicate how you intend to capture this market share, and the techniques and methods you will use.

This section can be the most difficult part of your business plan. Statistics on demographics can be obtained from your local government's statistics division. These statistics are obtained from census polling and government departments that track public expenditures.

Traditional a marketing strategy consists of three components, known as the "Three Cs":

- **Company:** Know the strengths and weaknesses of your pet business.
- **Competition:** Know the strengths and weaknesses of your competitors.
- **Customers**: Know who your customers are and what they want.

You need to identify your direct and indirect rivals, as well as gauge your potential fit in the marketplace. For example, if you want to open a brick-and-mortar location and not do online sales, direct competitors would be any other like-minded pet businesses operating in your geographic location and indirect competitors would be online pet businesses that are not in your geographical area.

Some issues to consider are your competitors' strengths and weaknesses, whether new competitors are entering the marketplace, or existing ones are leaving.

1.8 Sales and marketing strategy

The next step is to develop a marketing strategy, which involves analyzing the "Four Ps," collectively known as the marketing mix — from Marketing 101:

- **Product:** Describe the product you are selling.
- **Price:** Discuss how much you will charge for the product or service.
- **Place:** Talk about where you will sell your product or service.
- **Promotion:** Discuss special incentives you will use to get people to try your product. (See Chapter 5 for more information about promotions and marketing.)

Describe the method you will use for pricing your product or service. For example, what will be your mark-up on products? How will you decide? Will you accept cash, credit, debit, checks?

There are four pricing factors to consider for your service and product:

- What are the input costs (i.e., cost to offer the product)?

❧ What is the customer's perception of value? Will they see your product or service as high quality, medium, or low?

❧ What are your competitors charging for the same or similar offerings?

❧ What are your expected profit margins?

The marketing and competitive analyses are vital parts of your business plan and will likely be an extensive portion of it. Take the time to do thorough research on your competitors and how the market has behaved in recent and past years. A disorganized or unfocused marketing strategy can lead to disaster even for the best of companies.

1.9 Financial plan

The financial plan is the section that determines whether or not your business will be financially viable. It will determine whether or not your business plan is going to attract an investment.

The financial plan consists of three financial statements — the income statement, the cash-flow projection, and the balance sheet — and a brief explanation of these three statements.

To begin, divide the business expenses into two categories: your start-up expenses and your operating expenses. All the costs of getting your business up and running go into the start-up expenses category. These expenses may include business registration, starting inventory, rent deposits, down payments on property, equipment, utility deposits, furniture, and décor. This is just a small list of start-up expenses. There may be many more that you will add as you decide what you need to start.

All the costs of keeping your business running day-to-day are in the operating expenses category. Think of these as the things you're going to have to pay each month. Your list of operating expenses may include salaries (i.e., your salary and staff salaries), rent, telephone, utilities, advertising, and office supplies. Again, this is just a partial list to get you going.

1.9a Income statement

The income statement is one of the three financial statements that you will need to include in the financial plan section of your business plan. The income statement shows your revenues, expenses, and profits for a particular time period (see Worksheet 1).

On the CD that comes with this book, you will find an income statement that you can use for your business. Not all of the categories in this income statement will apply to your pet business so delete those that don't apply and add categories where necessary.

1.9b Cash-flow projection

The cash-flow projection shows how cash is expected to flow in and out of your business. For you, it's an important tool for cash-flow management, letting you know when your expenditures are too high or when you might want to arrange short-term investments to deal with a cash-flow surplus. As part of your business plan, a cash-flow projection will give you a much better idea of how much capital investment your business idea needs.

For a bank loans officer, the cash-flow projection offers evidence that your business is a good credit risk and that there will be enough cash on hand to make your business a good candidate for a line of credit or short-term loan.

Do not confuse a cash-flow projection with a cash-flow statement. The cash-flow statement shows how cash has flowed in and out of your business. In other words, it describes the cash flow that has occurred in the past. The cash-flow projection shows the cash that is anticipated to be generated or expended over a chosen period of time in the future.

While both types of cash-flow reports are important decision-making tools for businesses, we're only concerned with the cash-flow projection for the business plan right now. You will want to show cash-flow projections for each month over a one-year period as part of the financial plan portion of your business plan.

There are three parts to the cash-flow projection (see Worksheet 2). The first part details your *cash revenues*. Enter your estimated sales figures for each month. Remember that these are cash revenues; you will only enter the sales that are collectible during the specific month you are dealing with.

The second part is your *cash disbursements*. Take the various expense categories from your ledger and list the cash expenditures you expect to pay each month.

Worksheet 1
Income Statement

(Insert your business name.)
Income Statement for the year ending _____ October 31, 20-- _____

REVENUE	
Products	$51,290.90
Services	19,244.00
Total Revenue	70,534.90
EXPENSES	
Direct Costs	
Salary (Owner)	44,000.00
Wages	
Unemployment insurance	
Employment taxes	1,000.00
Mandatory government deductions (e.g., Federal Insurance Contributions Act, Canada Pension Plan)	6,040.00
Workers' Compensation	1,000.00
Other:	
Total Direct Costs	51,040.00
General and Administration	
Accounting and legal fees	
Advertising and promotion	200.00
Bank charges	
Depreciation and amortization (on equipment and building if you own it)	
Insurance	900.00
Interest	
Office rent	
Telephone	298.00
Utilities	
Credit card charges	
Office supplies	55.00
Property tax	
Security system	
Equipment, furniture, and renovations	
Other:	
Total General and Administration	1,453.00
Total Expenses	52,493.00
Net Income before Taxes	18,041.90
Income Taxes	2,886.70
Net Income	15,155.20

The third part of the cash-flow projection is the *reconciliation of cash revenues to cash disbursements*. As the word "reconciliation" suggests, this section starts with an opening balance, which is the carryover from the previous month's operations. The current month's revenues are added to this balance; the current month's disbursements are subtracted, and the adjusted cash-flow balance is carried over to the next month.

Remember, the closing cash balance is carried over to the next month. The main danger when putting together a cash-flow projection is being overly optimistic about your projected sales.

1.9c Balance sheet

The balance sheet is the last of the financial statements that you need to include in the financial plan section of the business plan (see Worksheet 3). The balance sheet presents a picture of your business's net worth at a particular point in time. It summarizes all the financial data about your business, breaking that data into three categories: assets, liabilities, and equity.

Once again, this template is an example of the different categories of assets and liabilities that may apply to your business. The balance sheet will reproduce the accounts you have set up in your general ledger. You may need to modify the categories in Worksheet 3 to suit your own business.

Once you have your balance sheet completed, you'll be ready to write a brief analysis of each of the three financial statements. When you're writing these analysis paragraphs, you want to keep them short and cover the highlights, rather than write an in-depth analysis. The financial statements themselves (i.e., income statement, cash-flow projection, and balance sheet) will be placed in your business plan's appendixes.

1.9d Start-up costs

In order to know what your start-up costs will be, you need to identify what your expenses will be in the beginning. Worksheet 4 will help you calculate your start-up costs. Think about equipment, advertising, office, and vehicle expenses. (All of these worksheets are available on the CD.)

You will also need to figure out where the money will come from if you don't have enough savings to begin your business.

Worksheet 2
Cash-Flow Projections

	January	February
Cash Revenues		
Revenue from product sales	$4,272.24	$4,272.24
Revenue from service sales	$1,603.67	$1,603.67
Total Cash Revenues	$5,877.91	$5,877.91
Cash Disbursements		
Cash payments to suppliers	$1,200.00	$1,200.00
Management draws	$3,000.00	$3,000.00
Salaries and wages	$100.00	$100.00
Promotional expenses		
Professional fees		
Rent or mortgage		
Insurance		
Telecommunications	$50.00	$50.00
Utilities	$30.00	$30.00
Total Cash Disbursements	$4,380.00	$4,380.00
Reconciliation of Cash Flow		
Opening cash balance	$10,000.00	$11,497.91
Add total cash revenues	$5,877.91	$5,877.91
Deduct total cash disbursements	$4,380.00	$4,380.00
Closing Cash Balance	$11,497.91	$12,995.82

1.10 Forecasts and projections

How do you see your business growing, expanding, or changing in future years? Investors, as well as yourself, will find it helpful to see how you envision your company evolving and reacting to the ever-changing market. The questions you will need to address in this section include:

- Does recent data show the market for your product is growing?

- Do you have a plan to offer new products or line extensions in the first few years?

- Are there other ways to position your company more competitively in the marketplace?

2. Revisit Your Business Plan

It is helpful to review your business plan at least once every six months for the first three years; after that, once a year is sufficient. It shows how close your projections are and if you are keeping to your plan. It is not a bad thing to change the plan or adjust it. Just make sure what you change coincides with your original plan and does not conflict as this may cause problems.

Worksheet 3
Balance Sheet

(Insert your company name.)
Balance sheet as of _____ October 31, 20-- _____ *(Date)*

ASSETS	
Current Assets	
Cash in bank	$10,000.00
Petty cash	590.00
Total net cash	10,590.00
Inventory	1,000.00
Accounts receivable	5,900.00
Prepaid insurance	600.00
Total Current Assets	**$18,090.00**
Fixed Assets	
Land	
Buildings	
Less depreciation	
Net land and buildings	
Equipment	$600.00
Less depreciation	100.00
Net equipment	500.00
Total Assets	**$500.00**
LIABILITIES	
Current Liabilities	
Accounts payable (including wages and salaries)	$3,000.00
Vacation pay	575.00
Unemployment insurance	200.00
Mandatory government deductions (e.g., FICA,CPP)	100.00
Federal income tax payable	100.00
Workers' Compensation	100.00
Pension payable	
Union dues payable	
Medical payable	57.50
Taxes charged on sales	79.00
Taxes paid on purchases	59.00
Taxes owing	138.00
Total Current Liabilities	**$4408.50**

Worksheet 3 — Continued

Long-Term Liabilities	
Long-term loans	
Mortgage	
Total Long-Term Liabilities	
Total Liabilities	$4,408.50
EQUITY	
Earnings	
Owner's equity — Capital	
Owner — Draws	
Retained earnings	
Current earnings	
Total Equity	
Liabilities + Equity	

Worksheet 4
Start-Up Costs

Start-Up Costs

Equipment	$ 500.00
Starting inventory	$ 1,000.00
Advertising	$ 200.00
Professional fees	$ 200.00
Office supplies	$ 100.00
Rent	$ 6,600.00 ← (for one year — $550.00 per month)
Land and/or buildings	$ —
Licenses	$ 100.00
Telephone	$ 50.00
Utilities	$ 100.00
Repairs	$ —
Leasehold improvements	$ 500.00
Vehicle expenses	$ —
Miscellaneous	$ 1,000.00
Other: _____	$ —
Total	$ 10,350.00

Sources of Capital

How will you raise the money for start-up expenses?

Owner investment	$ 10,000.00
Shareholders	$ 5,000.00
Loan monies	$ —
Lines of credit	$ 10,000.00
Savings	$ 5,000.00
Other: _____	$ —
Total	$ 30,000.00

Chapter 3

Setting up Your Business Structure and Obtaining Financing

Setting up your business structure and obtaining financing is easier when you have a well-thought-out business plan. This chapter will help you with the details and to consider the pros and cons of each business structure. Take your time and do your research on what will work for your business now and in the future.

When deciding on a business structure, it is advisable to seek advice from a business lawyer or business accountant.

1. Deciding on a Business Structure

When beginning a business, you must decide what form of business entity to establish. The most common forms of business structure are the sole proprietorship, partnership, corporation, and Limited Liability Company (LLC).

Legal and tax considerations should be taken into account when selecting a business structure for your business. Your form of business determines which income tax return form you have to file and the tax rate that will be applied. You can always change your business structure down the road, if required, although depending on the structure you choose initially it could be complicated.

1.1 Sole proprietorships

A sole proprietorship is the simplest business structure and more than likely one that you will use in the beginning. As a single owner, you will control the entire business and be responsible for all financial obligations. You will be responsible for keeping records of all the profits as well as paying all of the taxes. You are basically taxed on business earnings the same as you are taxed on wages or salaries earned as an employee for a company.

The advantages of a sole proprietorship are its simplicity and its minimal restrictions as well as the fact that it is very easy to establish and terminate a sole proprietorship.

The main disadvantage is the unlimited liability faced by the owner, which means if your business is sued, you may lose your personal assets

31

such as your house, vehicle, land, and investments. Another disadvantage for a sole proprietorship can be the difficulty in raising capital.

1.2 Partnerships

In a partnership each person contributes money, property, labor and/or skill, and expects to share in the profits and losses of the business. A partnership must file an annual information return to report the income, deductions, gains, losses, etc., from its operations, but it does not pay income tax. Instead, it "passes through" any profits or losses to its partners. What this means is that each partner includes his or her share of the partnership's income or loss on his or her personal tax return.

One of the advantages of a partnership can include the benefits of combining the knowledge of each of the partners' different areas of expertise. People always say "two heads are better than one"!

In the United States, each partner pays separate income taxes. This means less taxes per person at the end of the fiscal year.

With a partnership you are not the only one professionally or financially responsible which can be an asset in times of trouble. It's much easier to work through stressful periods when you're not the sole person responsible for making all the decisions. Two people's assets means more collateral, which is a plus, if you are going to require additional funding for your new pet business.

There are disadvantages, which can include a more complex business structure. For example, a partnership can require more finances to set up and dissolve (i.e., lawyer and accountant's fees) than a sole proprietorship.

Another disadvantage would be if you and your partner don't work well together. Unfortunately different ideas and goals can sometimes cause problems in the most stable of partnerships. What starts together also ends together so any choices you or your partner make individually will ultimately affect both of you. When mistakes are made, you will both suffer the consequences.

1.2a Partnership agreement

If you are going to have a partnership as your business structure, you should have a legal partnership agreement. The partnership agreement helps explain and define the roles of each partner. Note that in some areas in North America, you are required to have a written agreement.

Your partnership agreement should cover the following topics:

- Authority of each partner. You will want to define whether or not one partner is a silent partner, or if both partners will be involved in all the day-to-day operations, business decisions, and so forth.

- Money and time contributions of each partner. This is important so money doesn't become an issue right at the start. Clearly define who will pay what amount for start-up costs and investments as well as the amount of time each partner will contribute to the business.

- Division of profits and debts.

- Resolution of disputes. You need to include in your agreement how disputes will be resolved including whether or not a mediator will need to be consulted or whether one partner has veto power over the other partner(s).

- Provisions for retirement, succession, and death of each partner.

- How dissolution of the partnership will work.

- Partner salaries, compensation, and benefits.

- Buyout options if one partner wants to get out of the business.

- How the rights to business trademarks will be managed.

You should hire a lawyer to review your partnership agreement to make sure all the important information is covered in the agreement. In Canada, see *Partnership Agreement*, also published by Self-Counsel Press, for more information on this type of agreement.

1.3 United States corporations

According to the IRS (www.irs.gov, accessed September, 2011), "In forming a corporation, shareholders exchange money, property, or both, for the corporation's capital stock." When forming a corporation a board of directors must be established along with a president, secretary, etc.

A corporation can take special deductions that are not offered to sole proprietorships or partnerships. Again according to the IRS website,

"For federal income tax purposes, a C corporation in the United States is recognized as a separate tax-paying entity. A corporation conducts business, records net income or loss, pays taxes, and distributes profits to shareholders. The profit of a corporation is taxed to the corporation, and then is taxed to the shareholders when distributed as dividends.

"In the US, S corporations are corporations that elect to pass corporate income, losses, deductions, and credit through to their shareholders for federal tax purposes. Note that there are many restrictions on S corporations so consult with the Internal Revenue Service before incorporating as this type. Shareholders of S corporations report the flow-through of income and losses on their personal tax returns and are assessed tax at their individual income tax rates."

Keep in mind that if you incorporate your business, you will pay corporate taxes as well as personal taxes. The corporation does not get a tax deduction when it distributes dividends to shareholders. Shareholders cannot deduct any loss of the corporation but the shareholders and executive board cannot be held personally liable for any lost lawsuits.

The advantage to forming a corporation is limited personal liability protection for the owners (shareholders). This means that the corporation is held responsible for the debts, not the individuals, so you will not lose your personal property, investments, and savings. Another advantage is the perpetual existence independent of its shareholders; even if you pass away the corporation will continue to operate and exist.

The structure of a corporation allows the business to attract key and talented employees it may not be able to otherwise hire by offering an ownership interest in the form of stock options.

Some disadvantages of incorporation are the increased fees and costs such as professional fees to lawyers, accountants, and incorporation fees (these vary from state to state and province to province so be sure to research each accordingly). Another disadvantage is the adherence to the corporate formalities and paperwork. If the proper corporate formalities of organizing and running the corporation are not followed, the shareholders may lose the primary benefits of being a corporation (i.e., the limited personal liability protection originally sought).

Most new businesses begin as sole proprietorships or partnerships because it is less expensive. If you can't afford to start as a corporation, know that you may change your business structure down the road when you are ready to expand your business.

1.4 United States Limited Liability Company (LLC)

The IRS (ww.irs.gov, accessed September, 2011) says a Limited Liability Company (LLC) is a business structure allowed by US state statute. LLCs can be a great choice for smaller businesses because, similar to a corporation, owners have limited personal liability for the debts and actions of the LLC. In other words, if your company loses a lawsuit, the suing party cannot take your personal assets such as your house, land, and investments.

LLCs are structured similarly to partnerships, providing more management flexibility and the benefit of pass-through taxation method.

1.5 Incorporating in Canada

Incorporating in Canada may be more complicated and expensive than starting your business as a sole proprietorship or partnership. If this is your first business, you may want to start small; when you eventually expand your business, you could incorporate it.

The biggest disadvantage to incorporating is there are high start-up costs. You will also need to deal with other people such as shareholders, a board of directors, and officers. There are more documents to be filed, such as Articles of Incorporation, annual returns, notices of any changes to the board of directors, and changes to the address of your business's registered office. As a corporation, your business will also need to maintain certain corporate records, and file corporate income tax returns. All of this increases accounting fees as well.

If you don't have a lot of money to start your company, incorporating your business may be a way to get investments from shareholders. Shareholders buy shares into the company and then they are paid based on the percentage of shares or stocks they own in the company.

The advantage to incorporating is that your company will have limited liability. This means that you are personally protected from lawsuits and creditors. If your company goes bankrupt, your personal property and finances should be safe, unless you have provided personal guarantees for your company's debt. This means that you and the shareholders will not lose more than your investments in the company. Also, creditors cannot sue you or the shareholders for debts incurred by the corporation.

2. Business Licensing

In most areas, your business needs to be licensed to operate legally. Depending on your business, you may need to be licensed at the federal, state or provincial, and/or local level. Beyond a basic operating license, you may need specific permits, such as a zoning permit (see Chapter 4 for more information about zoning regulations).

Regulations vary by industry, state or province, and locally, so it's very important to understand the licensing rules where your business is located. Not complying with regulations can lead to expensive fines and can put your business at serious risk.

Visit your local federal office, its website, or phone them to get a listing of federal, state or provincial, and local permits, licenses, and registrations you'll need to run your business.

The website for the US government's business information site is www.usa.gov. The website for Canada's government's business site is Canada Business at www.canadabusiness.ca. These websites have everything you need to know about government regulations and business registrations and printable forms to help you with your business.

You will likely need a local business license. You will also need to register your business name with the state or province in which you are setting up your business. If you think you might go national, you will want to register your business name nationally as well.

3. Business Identification Number

Before you apply for a business identification number, you will need to decide on a business name, location, and legal structure, then register with the federal, state or provincial, and municipal (local) governments.

For filing payroll taxes with the Internal Revenue Service (IRS) you will need to acquire an Employer Identification Number (EIN), also known as the Federal Tax Identification Number. This will be your business tax ID number. The EIN assigned to your business will be used by the tax authorities to keep track of the amount of taxes you pay. Almost all businesses need an EIN. Registering for this number is a free service offered by the IRS.

In Canada, to file payroll taxes with Canada Revenue Agency (CRA), you will need to apply for a Business Number (BN). The BN is a nine-digit account number that identifies your business to federal and provincial governments and it helps them keep track of the amount of taxes you pay.

In the US, you may need to get a State Employer Identification Number (EIN) from the state in which you are doing business, so that the state government can also keep track of the amount of state taxes you're paying. The IRS will provide you with information about paying your employee federal and state taxes.

4. Business Bank Account

Having a separate account for your business makes accounting much simpler. Your business bank records will help you keep track of where your business is financially and help you to prepare business reports and tax returns. Assuming that at least some of your income will be gathered in the form of checks, a business account also simplifies deposits. Don't forget that all bank fees in your business account can be claimed as expenses on your tax returns.

Choosing a business account will depend on how often you make transactions, and what type of payments you accept. All banks have a different fee structure and you are likely to have to pay a fee for each deposit, withdrawal, and check although some banks and credit unions offer an inclusive-type package at a flat rate.

It is best to look at a number of accounts and compare them in terms of your own business needs. For instance, if your business will receive many checks and pay out money infrequently, an account with low-deposit fees will suit you better; a business receiving direct deposits and large payments may not worry about low-deposit fees if the monthly fee is low.

Think about the types of transactions you anticipate each month. Knowing this will allow you to make realistic comparisons between different accounts. Some factors to consider in choosing your business account include:

🐾 Monthly fees

🐾 Deposit fees, including additional charges for depositing checks

- Accessibility via tellers, ATMs, and online banking, or by phone
- Overdraft protection plan fees
- Withdrawal fees
- Convenience — Where is the nearest branch or the nearest ATM? Are there fees to transfer money to your personal account? What are the hours and days of the bank?
- Fees for money conversions if you expect overseas transactions

Once you have selected your account, you will need to visit the bank to get things started. Most business accounts require a business name search before they can be activated. This is to check that it is a legitimate business. To open an account you will need:

- Business name certificate (note that some banks want this, while others don't)
- Personal identification (e.g., license, passport, existing bank account details, health-care card, or a birth certificate)
- Money for an initial deposit; each bank will have a different minimum amount depending on the account features.
- A completed application form with the name, address, contact details, and birth date of each account holder

The business bank account should always be separate from your personal account. This will allow you to track business expenses and sales more accurately and with less effort. Also, if you incorporate your business, it is a legal requirement that you keep your personal and business bank accounts separate. Another reason is that if you ever get audited by the IRS or CRA it will allow for a more fluid process with less hassle and time explaining and proving that your purchases were for your business and not for you personally. Your accountant or bookkeeper will appreciate having the two bank accounts divided and it will result in less time to perform his or her tasks, which translates to fewer expenses for you.

5. Bookkeeping and Accounting

Even if you decide to hire a professional accountant or bookkeeper to perform your business finance tasks, you will need to maintain detailed records of all of your business transactions such as deposits, checks, expenses, and products and services sold. If you stay on top of your paperwork when it comes time to doing the actual bookkeeping or have a professional do it, it will not be such a daunting task. If you procrastinate, or don't stay organized, it will become a tedious job to find receipts, remember certain expenses, and find sales receipts when it comes to filing your taxes. A good habit to get into at least once a month is to balance all business expenses and revenues.

You will need to decide what type of bookkeeping system you are going to use. You have plenty of options to choose from such as computer programs (e.g., *Simply Accounting*), or an online system, or a point-of-sale system (e.g., cash register), or the old-fashioned method of a ledger book and cash box.

If you decide to use a computer program and hire an accountant, be sure that your accountant uses the same software as you or is at least familiar with it. Some computer programs come with functions that evaluate sales and expenses and offer reports that give insights to increased profitability. If you choose to hire an accountant, he or she can easily extract the information from your computer program to prepare payroll tax returns and analyze the data to evaluate your business goals. An accountant can also find tax loopholes for your business that you might not have known about, which will save you money or give you certain tax incentives.

When setting up your bookkeeping structure, make sure you are doing it in a manner that makes it easy for the accountant or bookkeeper to perform his or her tasks. You can do this by visiting your accountant before setting up your books and asking for his or her input; this can reduce costs significantly.

Bookkeeping can be difficult for a small business due to staff resources so remember to keep accurate and timely records. If you attend a pet convention remember to keep receipts for costs incurred such as hotels, food, etc., and record this in your bookkeeping ledger or computer system as soon as you return from the trip. Waiting can cause lost receipts and forgetting to record the incurred expenses at tax time.

6. Sales Tax

In the US, check with the IRS to be directed to each state's specific tax regulations. In addition to federal tax, you will be required to pay some state and local taxes, and each state and locality has its own set of tax rates.

Some of the more common types of state taxes are the state sales tax; income tax, which is the same as the federal income tax, just a different rate; and employment taxes, which is in addition to federal employment taxes in which the state requires the business to pay workers' compensation and unemployment insurance taxes. Some states even require a disability insurance tax.

In Canada, every province and territory requires businesses to collect a Goods and Services Tax (GST) on all products and services sold at a 5 percent rate. Some provinces have an additional sales tax on top of the GST called a Provincial Sales Tax (PST), or a combination of taxes called a Harmonized Sales Tax (HST). The rate varies from province to province.

Having knowledge of your state or provincial tax requirements can help you avoid problems and save your business money. For more information about taxes contact your local tax authority or consult with a business accountant.

7. Filing Tax Returns

In the US and Canada, the governments require your business records (whether in paper or electronic format) to be reliable and complete, and for you to provide the correct information needed to fulfill your tax obligations and to calculate your entitlements. Your returns should be supported by source documents that verify the information contained in the records; and include other documents, such as appointment books, logbooks, income tax and sales tax records, scientific research and experimental development (SR&ED) vouchers and records, and certain accountants' working papers, to assist in determining your obligations and entitlements.

Keep in mind that you are always responsible for your tax returns even if they are done by an accounting firm as you are the one that submits the sales and expenses information to your tax authority. It is recommended that you hire an accountant to prepare your tax returns as the information can be complicated as well as time intensive. Also, your accountant might know of certain tax loopholes which could help to lower your taxes or he or she may find tax incentives that could help your business.

8. Finding a Lender

Depending on which type of pet business you plan on opening you will more than likely require some form of financing. Finding financing can be a daunting task as most people do not have a large amount of savings to start a business. This is where your business plan will come into play significantly and help you to obtain investors or a business loan. It will determine which type of business structure you will have (i.e., sole, proprietorship, partnership, limited liability company, or corporation), which will help you decide how to approach lenders and investors.

It is critical to have your business plan well prepared before meeting with banks or investors. Any potential lender will want to make sure that he or she will get paid back the money lent to you, as well as interest, so be prepared for any questions the lender may ask you.

Any bank, financial lender, or investor will require that you personally contribute money to your business as well so be prepared to have some savings to contribute. If you are not investing any of your money, why would anyone else trust enough to invest their money in your business?

8.1 Banks and other financial lenders

The most common method used to obtain financing is to approach a bank or other financial lender. The bank will want to know how well you know your business, the positives and negatives, and why you will be successful at the endeavor. The more credentials, work experience, and volunteer experience you have in the area of the business you want to start, the more confident the lender will feel that your business will be profitable. If you do not have any experience, then maybe forming a partnership with someone who has the experience will help get the loan approved.

In some circumstances you can use your personal assets (e.g., your home) to secure a loan, which will be used as collateral. The downside to this is your home or other assets you used to obtain the loan can be taken by the bank if your business loan payments are not met.

A cosigner can also help get you a loan if he or she has good credit and collateral, but you may not find a lot of people willing to risk their assets and good credit rating for someone else's business.

If you have a poor credit rating, it will be more difficult to secure financing. If you do secure financing with poor credit, you will have higher interest rates attached to your loan.

To obtain your credit score contact a government-approved credit reporting agency. If your credit rating is bad, you should work on improving it before you attempt to acquire a business loan. This can be done by contacting the companies to which you owe money and setting up a reasonable payment plan so creditors can begin the process of removing bad records from your file; however, this can be a lengthy process. One more option is to look into government programs that assist people with bad credit or that offer business grants.

8.2 Financial investors

Another method of obtaining financing is to find investors. These are people or companies who will invest in your business idea in exchange for part ownership in your company and/or payouts from the profits. This can be a viable solution to avoiding bank loans with high interest rates but you will have to forfeit some of the decision making, because the investors will likely have a say in your business operations.

If you go with this option, it is advisable to have a lawyer involved to outline and document all decision-making power in regards to who makes which decisions and exactly what portion of the company will be owned by the investors as well as how and when payments will be made to investors.

8.3 Personal loans from friends or family

Personal loans from friends or family can be another way to get the money you need to start your business. This method will have less red tape and more than likely lower interest rates than a loan from a financial institution.

The downside to personal loans is they could result in a loss of a friendship or family relationship because of your inability to pay it back or being late on payments. When taking personal loans beware of the consequences and always have a lawyer draw up a loan agreement to avoid any confusion on loan-payment terms.

8.4 Grants

Grants or partial grants can be another option, especially if you're working in the nonprofit sector. Grants can provide you with needed financial assistance when looking to start your pet business.

Government agencies and some nonprofit organizations (e.g., Volunteers of America), can provide assistance with locating which foundations and lenders are accepting grant applications for your industry or innovation and how to apply for them.

Be especially aware of considerations within the granting system such as the parameters of the grant and the possibility of special funds given to ethnic minorities, women, or people with disabilities. Also be aware that applying for a grant does not guarantee you will receive it.

Chapter 4

Choosing a Location

hen it comes to the process of choosing a location for your new pet business there can be a lot of excitement. Many of my associates and colleagues have remarked that finding the location for their businesses was the definitive moment that made their entrepreneurial ventures a reality.

In this chapter we will focus on the more common locations for doing business: home-based businesses, leasing a commercial property, purchasing a commercial property or established business, or joining a franchise with specific locations.

1. The Home-Based Pet Business

Starting a home-based business is a viable, low-cost option for many who are just starting a new pet business venture. Some of the benefits of a home-based pet business include lower overhead costs because there is no second mortgage or rent to pay out for business space.

With a home-based pet business you can create your own schedule, and set your own hours; ergo you can put as much time as you feel is needed into your business. It is very important that your professionalism is never compromised no matter what type of location you choose for your business; keep that in mind if you choose to run a business from home. Make sure you are available to your clients by keeping a consistent schedule or using other approaches to get back to them quickly. Being based out of your home may be less formal, but it does not mean it is automatically any less professional than a business in a commercial or retail park.

Some considerations when starting a home-based pet business include designating an out-of-the-way area for the operation of your business during your business hours. It is very easy for family, friends, and household chores to cause distractions.

There is the benefit of tax breaks since home-based businesses are eligible to claim a portion of personal space as business or office area; for example, property tax, utilities, repairs and maintenance, home insurance, and an interest portion of mortgage or rent may all be tax deductible. Also, if for some reason you want to close the business, a home-based business would not be locked into a retail lease.

Be aware of your own expansion needs and future projections for your business. Keep in mind that depending on the size of your home or the space allotted for your pet business, expansion within a home-based business can be more difficult. Note that some pet services such as grooming or daycares may require your property to be zoned commercially. Depending on your area, it can be a time-consuming and expensive endeavor to get it rezoned. If zoning is not possible in the area you live, you will need a backup location plan in place.

Although home-based businesses make up about half of all US businesses (according to www.census.gov, accessed October 2011), many areas have significant entry barriers at the local level, with zoning laws and prohibitions. Most local zoning laws either restrict the type of businesses allowed to be conducted in residential areas or have banned commercial activity entirely unless the business receives an exception. When starting a home-based business, make certain you are aware of all zoning laws and prohibitions in your area.

Depending on your local laws, zoning rules may apply to physical changes and visibility, prohibiting exterior physical changes to the home for the purposes of conducting business as well as prohibiting outside business activities, storage, or displays, and the restriction of signage or commercial vehicles.

If there is traffic or parking zoning in your area, it could restrict the number of visitors to your home-based business. This could also affect the number of employees working in your home or prohibit employees altogether, and restrict business parking or require that additional parking be provided.

The most basic of zoning codes restrict or prohibit nuisance impacts (e.g., noise, odors) and restrict business activities. Many zoning codes prohibit certain types of businesses in residential areas. In some cases, zoning restrictions may exist for different types of business within residential areas. Also, in some jurisdictions, complying with zoning restrictions may include applying for and then obtaining a permit.

Make sure you have a basic understanding of local zoning ordinances by visiting your local zoning office. Zoning laws are determined by your city or municipal government. Find out which government agency enforces your zoning laws, and learn the specific laws that apply to operating a home-based pet business.

Remember to check local, state or provincial, and federal regulations for health, safety, and taxation regulations before you start operating any business from your home.

2. Leasing Commercial Property

Having a business on commercial property can offer public visibility and easy access. Many pet business owners choose a commercial base because there is a sense of permanency as well as the fact that the land is already zoned for commercial use. Depending on how you market your public image the right space could be a stepping stone in terms of delivering that image.

When you have found what you think is the perfect space for your new pet business, you are ready to sit down and negotiate the lease. There are certain items you will need to consider. The first item of business is usually the cost of the lease itself. Lease costs are determined by two factors:

1. The monthly cost is generally determined by multiplying the square footage by the cost per square foot, which gives you the annual cost, then dividing by 12 for the monthly cost. For example, a retail space of 3,000 square feet, at $25 a square foot, the annual cost would be $75,000, divided by 12 for a monthly cost of $6,250.

2. Common area maintenance (CAM) costs are added on to the monthly cost. If you are leasing a space in a commercial building or strip-mall area, the CAM costs are those "general" building areas such as walkways, parking lots, green areas, hallways, and, in some cases, restrooms. When leasing in a commercial space such as a mall, maintenance of common areas such as courtyards, and mall advertising, may also be added to the leasing price. It is similar to fees for residential property such as condominiums; you may get the extra commodities and "wow" factor, but be prepared to pay for it.

Before you sign the lease, review the document with an attorney to be sure that you understand everything to which you are agreeing. Be aware of the fine print. If the lease agreement is too convoluted, don't be afraid to take it to your lawyer and ask questions. Know exactly what will be covered and what is included. Remember you can negotiate a lease so don't settle on things that can be easily changed at no cost to yourself. Once the lease is signed it is binding.

2.1 Additional costs

The next topic of discussion should be what additional costs are included in the lease. These costs typically include property taxes; snow removal; lawn mowing; landscaping; and driveway, sidewalk, and parking lot repairs and maintenance. It may also include garbage collection, property insurance, and structural repairs and replacements. Typically in North America, nonstructural repairs and maintenance are the responsibility of the tenant's, as well as mechanical system repairs, maintenance, and replacements. For example, if your hot water tank fails, or your furnace quits working, it may be your responsibility to fix it. Make sure the lease agreement outlines which of these items are included in the lease payment, and which items you will be responsible for replacing or repairing if they break down.

2.2 Renovating leased property

Unless someone with a pet business exactly like yours was the previous tenant, you will probably need to have some changes made to the leased space before you start occupying. There may also be repairs that need to be made, or larger renovations done to make the space acceptable to your particular pet business. In some cases, the landlord may require that a professional contractor do the work. Who will pay for this work is an important question that needs to be negotiated.

As well, you should have outlined for you what is defined as leasehold improvements. Additionally, the lease should specify what happens to the improvements when the lease ends. Some leases may ask for you to pay to have your leasehold improvements removed at the end of the lease term at your expense.

Pay special attention to the "use of space" clause. This needs to be as broad as possible. Too narrow a use clause may mean that if your pet business changes focus, or you wish to expand into another area, the landlord has the option to object, leaving you to look for a new location.

2.3 Time period

The term of the lease should also be discussed. Landlords like long-term tenants so the longer the lease, the more concessions you may be able to negotiate in terms of renovations or other costs. Try to negotiate a bonus for staying on as a tenant for a certain amount of years or for renewing your lease a certain amount of times.

Should you find future expansion of your business requires you to change your location you want be sure that you can sublease the space under terms that are favorable to you and your business. When negotiating, ensure that the lease allows you to sublet without restrictive conditions. With good negotiation you may be able to negotiate lease termination so that if you no longer need the space, you are able to opt out of your lease entirely. This may be tied to a lump-sum penalty, or a percentage penalty based on how many months or years are left on your lease.

When looking at renewal options, ensure that you are not stuck paying the same amount you initially negotiated, especially if rent has decreased in your area. If the original lease states you do have to pay the same amount, there is no room for negotiation at the end of your term. On the reverse side of that, if you sign a lease that locks you in at a certain rate even if property values increase, your rent will be the same.

2.4 Other considerations when signing a lease

If you are looking to lease in a strip mall, or larger commercial office building, the landlord may require that your potential neighbors approve your business and agree to be your neighbor before you can sign the lease. When leasing in a mall not only will you be subject to a review by a commercial board or committee who oversees all tenants of the mall, you will be subject to their terms of operation as well.

Your discussion with the landlord should also include questions about other aspects of the lease, such as restrictions on signage. For example, if you're thinking of leasing in a historical district, signage may have to be approved by a historical society or committee and the landlord. This will require extra time and expenses on your part, although sometimes government money is available for historical upgrades.

3. Purchasing an Established Business

There are pros and cons to purchasing an established business. Some of the pros include:

- An established business can mean an established clientele.

- Move-in-ready pet businesses may have virtually no start-up requirements.

- Marketing and trademarks are already established which means you can choose to continue with the previous owner's methods if his or her business has been profitable.

- An understanding of what your potential revenues and expenses will be. This is helpful if you will be seeking a loan or investors to help you purchase your "new to you" pet business.

The good reputation of an established business may mean you'll spend less on common start-up costs (e.g., advertising and promotions), allowing you to focus more on other aspects of income generation, such as the creation of an online catalog or "new ownership" promotions.

If you intend to purchase a business at which you frequently shop, you may already have ideas regarding new products or merchandise not being carried by the current owners. Chances are if you've looked for a product, so have other people.

Some negative aspects of purchasing an established pet business could be the reason the current owners are choosing to sell their business. For example, what is the current financial state of the business? If the current owners are not making a profit, you will need to review their previous income and expense statements to find out why, and for how long this has been going on. Figure out whether or not you can have an impact on the current retail market with a few changes or if it will take a lot of time and money to make many changes. What will it take to turn the existing business around? Is the effort too great? Is the current location a factor?

Always look at any and all reasons as to why the owners are selling. Their old problems can quickly become your new problems. If their particular market is based on a current trend, how long will that trend last, and can you improvise and adapt, if necessary? For example, there is one particular business currently operating as a pet-friendly bed and breakfast in British Columbia. It opened in 2003 as a bed and breakfast focusing on environmentalism and outdoor adventure; it then changed focus to become an artists' retreat; finally it became a pet-friendly wilderness retreat in 2011. By adapting their business plan and adjusting their target market, the owners have been able to reinvent their business to cater to more than one source of revenue.

General questions to answer when looking at purchasing an established business include:

- Is the current owner in a partnership or is he or she a sole proprietor?

- Are you purchasing an incorporated business? If so, what dividends are expected to be paid to the previous owners and for how long?

- Does the business have a lease-to-own option or would it be a standard purchase?

- Do the current owners own the building or land in which the pet business currently resides? Is the building for sale or are you expected to move?

Thoroughly research any established business before you agree to commit to anything. If you are not sure of some of your findings consult a business lawyer or an accountant.

4. Joining a Franchise

When looking to operate a pet business, existing or new, another consideration would be whether or not to buy into a franchise. According to the Canadian Franchise Association, in 2011, the United States and Canada dominate the franchise industry the world over, and franchise businesses account for almost 50 percent of all retail sales in the United States and Canada. Also, franchising is the preferred Canadian small-business expansion model, as approximately one out of five consumer dollars are spent on goods and services at a franchise. Although sources vary on these numbers, listed are a few economic statistics regarding franchises in the United States and Canada:

- The franchise industry in Canada represents more than $100 billion CAD in sales annually and continues to grow.

- Average franchise fee per month: $23,000 CAD

- Average franchisee investment: $160,000 CAD
- Of all the franchises opened in Canada within the last five years, 86 percent are under the same ownership as when they opened, and 97 percent are still in business.
- The annual payroll for franchises in the United States is more than $229 billion USD.
- Franchising produces $1.53 trillion USD in total economic output in the United States.
- Total sales by franchised businesses are expected to reach more than $2 trillion USD (in 2011).
- In 2000, the median gross annual income, before taxes, of US franchisees was in the $74,000 USD to $125,000 USD range, with more than 30 percent of franchisees earning more than $149,000 USD per year.

These are just some general statistics to provide you with an idea of why so many small-business owners look to franchising as a business approach.

It is important to remember not all franchises are created equally. They may follow a similar pattern of operations, but how they carry out their day-to-day operations can vary greatly.

Some details to pay attention to when considering whether or not to join a franchise include:

- What are the franchise fees and regulations?
- What will you be expected to pay and when?
- Will you be paid a dividend payment or given stock options offered to those who purchase a franchise, and what portion of the payment is expected up front?

This will vary also according to whether or not your buy-in option includes a grace period for transfer of ownership or not. It is important to figure out what franchise fees will entail and to understand that they are separate from the initial fees you pay to become part of the franchise.

Find out how long the franchise has been in existence, and discern what its reputation is in other locations. Talk to other owners, ask them about their experiences with the franchiser. If the majority of them say they would do it all again, chances are you've found a responsible franchise.

Determine beforehand to which demographic the franchise caters, and whether it has a local, national, or international reputation. If the franchise is a household name across North America, you will have a lot less promotional work to do when opening your business. Some franchises even cover the costs of grand-opening promotions and marketing as part of the franchise agreement. If the franchise is not already a household name, find out if it plans to be.

Franchise expansions can have both negative and positive results on current franchisees, so be aware of all future expansion goals of any franchise you are looking at joining. It is also recommended that you know where the franchise head office is located and as much as possible about its background when assessing franchises.

Be friendly from the start with your corporate liaison because he or she will be your way of communicating to those who make the big decisions regarding franchise rules and regulations. For example, a logo or product change will affect your business in some aspect and, depending on the franchise, you may or may not have a say when changes are being made.

Many franchises retain all rights to merchandise and purchasing. Therefore, the products you carry can be changed or eliminated even if they are selling well at your store. Some companies, but not all, allow franchisees to request to carry different products but even these must be passed or approved by the franchise head office. Some are very strict and everything including your store decorations must be purchased through a specific company to guarantee that everything bearing the franchise name is consistent in every aspect.

Franchise laws and rules will vary from state to state, province to province, and franchise to franchise, so be certain to do your research thoroughly on any company you wish to join. Be aware of any and all laws and limitations should you ever choose to sell your franchised pet business; some franchises require payments even if you go out of business or you are losing money.

Interview a potential franchise the way you would a potential employee. Ask questions that will identify whether the franchise matches your personal objectives for your business, your ethics, and your ideals.

5. Buying Commercial Property

Once you have your budget in place, depending on your financial situation, you will have to decide whether buying business property is appropriate. With purchase you will be able to write off mortgage fees as a business cost, have equity in your investment, and be your own landlord, securing longevity in your location.

The downside would be that you would also be responsible for any hidden costs such as renovations or repairs to the site. If major structural changes need to occur to facilitate your pet business, do you have the budget to support extra, uncalculated expenses? It is highly recommended that you seek the advice of a property inspector and a local contractor to know what you are getting into before any purchase is made.

Once you have chosen a commercial building realtor, secured a mortgage, and found your property, you may make an offer. If the offer is accepted, a deposit is due. It is important to make sure everything you expect with your property is included in that final offer. Once you (the buyer) have signed the document, it becomes legally binding. If you withdraw from the offer at this stage, you may lose your deposit and you may also be sued.

Always make the final sale contingent on a building inspection and that you as the buyer are able to meet your financial obligations. Once your offer is complete it will be presented to the seller and negotiations may be made. They may include changes in price, possession date, and items included with the sale. The changes are initialled by the seller and returned to you (the buyer) for your initials. The resulting agreement of purchase and sale will state the purchase price and the deposit. The deposit is placed in a trust account and is credited toward the purchase price. When the offer has been accepted by both the seller and the buyer, the transaction is complete.

According to Assignments Canada (September, 2011), financing is typically available at 75 percent of the purchase price over a 25-year term. Each borrower's application is considered on a case-by-case basis. Ask your realtor about suitable mortgage brokers.

The mortgage approval may take approximately 24 to 48 hours after application and documentation has been submitted to the lender. The documentation required is generally income verification, tax returns, credit bureau or bank's report (letter from borrower's own bank stating that all accounts are in good standing to date), down payment confirmation via bank statements, copies of two pieces of government identification, and a real estate appraisal. The borrower will require the services of a lawyer or notary public to prepare the mortgage documents and registration at the Land Title or equivalent office in your area.

When interest rates are at historically low levels, many business owners consider the purchase of commercial real estate for their business locations. The benefits and drawbacks to commercial real estate ownership vary from business owner to business owner but potential buyers should educate themselves about the obvious and sometimes hidden benefits to the ownership of a commercial property.

Unlike residential loans, many commercial loans are assumable. This may make a business location and real estate much easier for you to acquire. Real estate would enhance the equity of your pet business.

For many pet business owners one of the primary benefits of commercial real estate ownership is that tax deductions can be taken on the interest portion of the monthly commercial loan payment. These deductions can be substantial and you should consult a qualified tax specialist about your unique situation. On average, commercial real estate properties have been said to appreciate about 2 to 3 percent above inflation over the long term. This equity appreciation can result in significant financial gains over a long period of time.

As many small-business owners will not receive a pension when they decide to retire, having a commercial property to sell can be that security. The equity appreciation on commercial property can be significant over a 10- or 20-year period. Business owners can decide either to sell their property at retirement, cashing in on equity appreciation, or lease it to another business for a continuous retirement income. In fact, in many situations, business owners may be able to lease an unused portion of their property, such as a spare office, before retirement for additional income.

Great fixed-rate loans for terms up to 30 years are now available for owner-occupied commercial properties in the United States. In some instances, with strong financials, a business owner may qualify for loan financing up to 100 percent of the purchase price for his or her commercial real estate.

In addition to the easily tangible benefits outlined above, by purchasing a commercial business property you would be able to pay back into the equity of your business each month rather than pay a landlord's mortgage.

Make certain that the property you purchase meets all legal and health standards required for operating your specific pet business. Always check local and federal legislation to ensure you are operating legally in every way. The last thing you want to do is purchase or open a new business only to have it shut down because you did not check into the local laws.

As the owner of the property and the business, all renovations, repairs, and unexpected costs fall on your shoulders, unless you have a partner or investors, so account for unexpected costs in your business plan.

Whether to buy or lease will be different for each individual situation and it really comes down to numbers and the level of commitment you wish to take on in the beginning. Review all options carefully before signing anything, especially when you are just starting your business.

6. Laws and Bylaws

Laws and bylaws need important consideration by anyone wishing to start a pet business. Be aware of legislation at all levels including federal, state or provincial, and local. Not only do you have to be aware of those regulations directly involving or regarding animals, but also those that could affect the type of business you wish to start.

6.1 Zoning regulations

Although this topic was covered briefly in section 1., it deserves further consideration. Zoning could affect the pet business you wish to start, depending on the type of pet business and your location.

Zoning typically governs what type of businesses can operate in a certain location or area. Commercial businesses are governed by similar but not as stringent regulations and restrictions as home-based businesses. Read the fine print as each piece of legislation is worded differently, from state to state and province to province.

Seek the proper definitions for what constitutes any regulations or exemptions. For example, I remember when the Lethbridge and District Humane Society wanted to take its organization to the next level and build a residence for its rescued animals. It had to purchase property in the industrial section of the city, in accordance with the local noise bylaws. The bylaws also stipulated that the residence had to be located away from residential areas.

6.2 Breeding bans

It is recommended that you be aware of current legislation regarding all animals in your area before starting your business plan. Some municipalities have specific bylaws pertaining to animals that actually prohibit the use or ownership of certain species and breeds. This is commonly referred to as Breed Ban Legislation. For example, in 2004 New Brunswick's Bill 55, *Restricted Dogs Act*, targeted the ownership of protective breed dogs (e.g., Staffordshire Bull Terriers, American Staffordshire Terriers, Rottweilers, or Akita Inus).

In some municipalities these breeds of dog are not welcome at all, permit or not. After much dispute and strong positions from both sides of all jurisdictions in the United States and Canada, some areas do have the right to enact breed-specific legislation. It is the attempt of this type of legislation to prevent the instances of attacks and injuries by restricting, regulating, or outright banning the ownership of powerful dog breeds.

Often this legislation includes mandatory spaying and neutering for all dogs of protective breeds, mandatory microchip implants, and liability insurance. It may mean prohibiting people convicted of a felony from owning them, comprehensive "dog bite" legislation, or mandating responsible pet ownership in some other way.

In the cases where breed-specific legislation does not ban breeds entirely but strictly regulates the conditions under which specific breeds can be owned, legislation is likely constantly being revised and could in the future include specifying public areas from which they would be prohibited, and establishing conditions, such as requiring a dog to wear a muzzle when in public places.

6.2a Breed-specific legislation in the United States

Breed-specific legislation is something to consider when opening any pet business in the United States. It could impact your future business if more breeds are included in the legislation.

Some jurisdictions have enacted breed-specific legislation in response to a number of well-publicized incidents involving pit bulls or other dog breeds commonly considered powerful. This legislation ranges from outright bans on the possession of these dogs to restrictions and conditions on ownership, and often presumes that these particular breeds are "dangerous" or "vicious." In response, some state-level governments have prohibited or restricted the ability of municipal governments within those states to enact breed-specific legislation.

According to www.canadasguidetodogs.com (accessed September 2011), Breed-specific laws were initially created to regulate pit bulls. This class of dogs is comprised of the following breeds: American Pit Bull Terrier, American Staffordshire Terrier, and Staffordshire Bull Terrier. The American Bulldog is also starting to be classified within this group. They share a common gene pool and have been crossbred with pit bulls for many years.

Although pit bulls are by far the most notable, several US cities have expanded breed-specific laws to incorporate additional powerful breeds, including: Dogo Argentino, Tosa, Fila Brasileiro, Cane Corso, Presa Canario, and Presa Mallorquin. Cities all across the US have enacted breed-specific legislation.

Although most of these restrictions apply to powerful breeds of dogs, there are many animals that are simply illegal to purchase, sell, or possess in certain states. It is important to research which species are considered restricted or exotic in your local area before opening a pet business.

If you're planning on opening an exotic animal reserve, make sure you are not violating any laws or legislations. Make sure all proper permits for working with restricted animals are obtained. Be aware of the reasons they are considered restricted, as many of them are restricted because of health regulations and it could mean a revocation of your business license if you have worked with certain animals or had them in your business location. On the plus side, if you know your legislation well, you can possibly use this information to your business's advantage, by always following the rules and keeping one step ahead of current regulations.

Research the current legislation in your area and surrounding locations. Also be aware of any upcoming legislation or pending amendments to current laws. After all, if your business goal is to start a Rottweiler-based pet business and your municipality drafts and passes breed-ban legislation six months after start-up, all your time, effort, and money would be lost.

6.2b Breed-specific legislation in Canada

Although the Canadian federal government does not regulate pit bull-type dogs, one provincial government and some municipal governments have enacted breed-specific legislation specifically banning or restricting pit bull-type dogs. For example, as of 2005, the province of Ontario's breed-ban legislation says that no person shall —

❧ own a pit bull;

❧ breed a pit bull;

❧ transfer a pit bull, whether by sale, gift, or otherwise;

❧ abandon a pit bull other than to a pound operated by or on behalf of a municipality, or a designated body;

❧ allow a pit bull in his or her possession to stray;

❧ import a pit bull into Ontario; or

❧ train a pit bull for fighting.

It further goes on to state that pit bulls are "grandfathered" if they were owned by an Ontario resident on August 29, 2005, or the dog was born in Ontario within 90 days after August 29, 2005. These dogs are subject to strict regulation and control, including the following:

❧ They must be muzzled and kept on a leash no more than 1.8 meters long when in public or when not on enclosed property.

❧ They must be spayed or neutered unless a veterinarian certifies the dog is physically unfit to be anesthetized.

❧ They will automatically be euthanized if a court finds they have bitten, attacked, or posed a menace, or if their owners are found to be in violation of the law or a related court order.

❧ Their owners are entirely liable for any and all damage caused by a bite or an attack.

If you have a pit bull puppy enter your pet business in Ontario, you are expected to notify authorities of its presence. Failure to do so could cause personal legal repercussions and you could risk the loss of your business. Again, know the legislation specific to your area — inside and out — before you put in a lot of time and effort creating your pet business.

Chapter 5

Marketing and Advertising Your Business

our marketing plan helps you think through the way you will get your business name out to your clients and establish the way the public will perceive your business. A good marketing strategy will build a solid foundation for your business, giving you a chance to prove why customers or clients should choose you over your competition.

Your marketing choices will define your business to your clients; the image you want to portray to the public will be reflected in the marketing plan decisions you make. Marketing is not just advertising, it is creating an image for your product and service and a method to effectively deliver that message to the public.

1. Identifying Your Target Market

Identify your target market by attempting to engage both the pets and their owners. Yes it is the owners who will be paying, but at the end of the day if the pets are happy, the owners are happy.

Know your target market before you create your marketing plan. Look at the various local demographics, identify who your particular pet business will appeal to most, and focus most of your energies on them. Demographic questions to consider:

🐾 What age range is your target market?

🐾 What is their income range?

🐾 What is their education level?

🐾 Where does your target market shop currently?

The answers to these questions will be very helpful. A lot of this information can be obtained through government statistics departments for your area.

Research the current trends and spending patterns of your target market by frequenting similar businesses. This can help you determine the direction your marketing plan should go. Once you have identified the population you wish to target, you can determine what price they are willing to pay; this will help with the pricing of your products and services.

You will need to decide where your particular business venue will be and what services and products you will be selling. You will also need to consider what makes your product and services unique, and help you stand out from your competition. Ideally you should be able to project the "what" in a short mission statement or tag line. For example, the PetSmart logo has the term "happiness in store" right below its business name. This is part of PetSmart's marketing plan in which it tries to send a happy feeling associated with the business. It is applied in PetSmart's advertising, store location, décor, the products offered, and even in its employee training manuals.

Choose something that will appeal to your target market. If you are selling a retail product, consider what is unique about it or what sets it apart from the other products on the market. If you are offering a pet service, what makes your service better or different from the competition? How will the service or product be offered, packaged, and presented? Remember that your marketing plan should be cohesive and all flow together. For example, you would not want to sell higher priced boutique-style pet items with a marketing plan that has more of a big-box store approach to it.

Where is your business location, and who will your business serve? Don't be afraid to associate yourself with a local landmark or historical site. Highlight easy-to-locate landmarks near your pet business when giving directions. This will give people a sense of familiarity even when you are just starting out.

You will need to consider where your target market is located. Choose a location that matches the service or product you are selling. If you are offering, for example, a service such as rehabilitation services for animals, you want a clean, safe, easily accessible location with parking, possibly close to a veterinarian's clinic. If you are in a tourist-filled location, you might use a different means of reaching your target market as tourists are only there for a short amount of time and come from many different locations. The location of the clients you want can influence the method used to reach them.

2. How to Reach Your Clients

The key to reaching your clients is to be creative. Marketing is not just about advertising, it is about creating a brand and image for your pet business. Once you know who your target market is follow them to where they are spending their money and find out what they are buying. Use this information to create a strategic marketing plan that targets your specific market.

You will also need to identify what types of media are reaching your target market. Find this information by contacting government agencies that provide statistics identifying the spending patterns and disposable income of your target market.

3. Marketing Goals

Your marketing goals should be attainable and realistic. It would be great to blanket your city or town with your business name on the radio or television, but that would cost thousands of dollars. You could hire a company to produce your business logo or slogan and an advertising campaign, but this can also be expensive. When you are just starting your business, you should consider inexpensive advertising and marketing alternatives first. Make your money count and be creative.

How many people do you want to reach with your marketing plan? Can you reach them all or will you have to focus on a select group within your target market? Perhaps you can stagger your marketing efforts over a selected period of time.

Your marketing goals should include some community involvement because this will increase awareness of your business thus translating to more sales and a good reputation within the community. Also, community involvement usually does not require large amounts of money.

If you are selling pet products that are natural or organic, you might want to have a recycling program at your business; this can be used as a marketing tool that is inexpensive as well as socially responsible, fit with the rest of the marketing plan, and help clients identify with your values.

4. Types of Advertising

Advertising would fall within the "promotions" part of the marketing plan and includes many different venues and methods. With any type of advertising you want to draw in the public. You need to give them important information but not too much information as this will confuse them or cause them to forget most of the message. Be sure to include contact information and something visually appealing to help your message stick in your clients' minds.

When dealing with advertising representatives be wary as they will entice you with many promises and deals; keep in mind that they are trying to make a living as well and most advertising representatives work on a commission basis. That being said, you will find some representatives will have good advice on how to target your market better.

Media such as radio and television can be expensive and may only hit a small percentage of your target market. If this option interests you, you could look at advertising in specialty, smaller media such as university or college radio stations or local television stations. You can also try to submit informational articles to newspapers and magazines (also called "service pieces") — sometimes these are published at no charge.

Remember to track where your clients are coming from. This can be done when you open your business. You can ask your clients where they heard about your business. This will let you know which advertising mediums are actually bringing in the clients. For example, if only 2 percent of your clients discovered your business from reading a newspaper advertisement, but 60 percent discovered your business through an online advertisement, it may be a good idea to drop the expensive newspaper advertising and focus on more online advertising.

4.1 Online advertising

Start creating awareness of your business before you open by using online resources. This can be a very effective way to create a buzz for your products and services before you even open your doors.

Facebook and other social networks offer free interactive ways to reach your clients and let them know about your business. Other sites include Twitter and pet-related websites such as BringFido.com.

Make sure that you open on the day you stated on any online sites. Delays in a grand opening can cause loss of interest by the public and build a negative image right from the start. A good way to gain interest is to offer a discount or deal to followers or fans of your social network site. For example, you could offer them deals during the first week you are open or to the first 20 or 100 customers.

Post lots of pictures online, whether you're using your own website, blog, Facebook account, or other location, and keep adding new information as this increases the chances that your followers will continue to view your online content.

Working with and around animals can cause emotions to run high at times. Never use a designated business group to post personal feelings or opinions. Discuss new developments in the industry, new laws, and new regulations pertaining to pets as well as some of the history of your industry and the animals to which you are catering. Pictures of new products and exciting new services or advances in the field can keep readers returning for more information.

If you or your employees have any training or certifications, put this information on the site and post any new accomplishments pertaining to the business. It is a good idea to update sites, blogs, Twitter, etc., at least once a week to keep things fresh and interesting.

4.1a Websites

A good website is a very important tool for your business even if you open a physical shop. With the invention of smart phones and other items such as the iPad, more than ever people are researching businesses online before even setting foot in the door. Your website should be clear, and easy-to-use so mobile devices can also connect with your business online.

Make sure you include contact information, a location and map, pictures, and information about your services and products. You want your website to have a professional feel to it, not a template feel. If you don't have the skills to create a good website for your business, you should consider hiring a website designer.

There are websites such as BringFido.com and SimplyPets.com on which you can advertise your business. These websites are dedicated to pet lovers and offer information on things such as pet-friendly restaurants, hotels, etc. Make sure their demographics match your target market.

Make sure all information is spell-checked before posting and try to ensure that your website loads quickly. People find slow loading websites annoying and usually will not wait for them to finish loading.

4.1b Blogs

Blogging can be an effective tool for those who have a lot of information to share, but again be professional at all times. Keep your posts short and informative. Too little information and infrequent postings will cause you to lose followers; too much information and too many posts will overwhelm and possibly even bore your readers. Check out other blogs by people in your industry to see what they are doing. If they have a lot of followers, chances are they are doing something right with their blogs.

Do not use your blog only to advertise your products and services as it will seem that your site is only about marketing your product. The trick is to keep followers interested in what you have to say, which makes them respect your business and want to buy things from you. For example, if you are selling dog boutique high-end clothing, include a picture of the new clothing you are promoting with a short story or historical fact on why owners started dressing their dogs.

Remember to include contact information and a link to your website from your blog.

4.2 Flyers and posters

Flyers and posters can be a low-price method of advertising depending on the method used to deliver them. You can buy and use mailing lists for specific areas from list brokers, the US Postal Service, or Canada Post, which can help make your advertising more effective and precise. This method can be an expensive technique but can be very effective.

Posters can be taken to other businesses for display and put up on community billboards. Hang door-hangers or place flyers in mailboxes, but be sure to respect no soliciting signs. With permission, civic centers, universities, colleges, coffee shops, and grocery stores may let you put up a poster.

Again make the posters, flyers, or door-hangers easy to read, and visually appealing. Most importantly, include your business contact information.

4.3 Cross promotions

Cross promoting can be an extremely cost-effective way to advertise your business with established businesses as well as align with another business's image. Go to businesses in your community or online and ask if they would like to join you in promoting both your business and theirs. For example, they put up a poster or your business cards, or place a logo on their website, in exchange for you doing the same with their information. This is an effective method of getting your name out there at the start.

When choosing a business to cross promote with, be careful to choose a business with a similar marketing plan and business ethics. Try to find businesses that are selling their product or service to the same clients you want to have but not with the same product or service you are selling.

4.4 Word of mouth

Do not discount word of mouth, especially within the pet community. Many of your customers may be connected through agility or training clubs, dog parks, and other pet-related venues and they will discuss their experiences with pet services and products. If they have had a good experience with your product or service, these happy clients can be your best and least expensive form of advertising. The key is to make sure your clients are happy.

Be careful how you treat your clients because research has shown if customers have a negative experience, they are likely to tell eight or more people about it; if they have a good experience, they will likely only tell two to three people.

4.5 Community and charity events

Sponsoring nonprofit charity events is a great way to get your name out there. People love a good cause and tend to more regularly frequent businesses that sponsor or are involved with charity and community events.

Being a part of this type of event usually costs a small donation, either of money or your product or service, but in return you get your business's name out to the community. Events like these are usually advertised by the event coordinators in local newspapers, on radio stations, and on television stations, and your business will be promoted as one of the sponsors. If the event is giving out merchandise such as T-shirts, hats, etc., your logo may be attached to them.

If your target market is adults who are 30 to 50 with children, you might consider sponsoring a youth sports team as kids' parents are usually at the games — especially the tournaments. You could also donate to local police and fire departments through a fundraiser to gain awareness and a good reputation for your business.

5. Cost Analysis for Advertising and Promotion

When analyzing your advertising and promotional costs, keep everything clear and concise. Make sure all components fit together. Review your plan often to ensure your marketing strategies are continually effective.

Think about how you plan to market your product or service. You will need to answer the following questions:

🐾 Do you have plans to attend trade shows or place ads in trade magazines?

🐾 Will you produce flyers to distribute to the public?

🐾 Do you have any ideas for an advertising campaign?

🐾 Do you have a plan in place to gain free publicity to create awareness about your product?

Determine a time line (i.e., what months will this action take place) and a budget for the first year of promotion. Worksheet 5 is a cost analysis to help you prepare a budget for your marketing. Research potential costs of the advertising and promotions you want to do in your first year, keeping in mind that you may want to start by doing the small and free things with your start-up budget. This form is included on the CD for you to use.

Worksheet 5
Cost Analysis for Advertising and Promotions

Action	Cost
Advertising	$ —
Radio	$ —
Newspaper	$ 800.00
Brochures or door hangers	$ —
Public relations	$ —
Pet expos	$ —
Trade shows	$ 500.00
Specialized packaging	$ —
Internet	$ 1,200.00
Other	$ —
Total	$ 2,500.00

Month	Promotional Activities	Cost
January	Google ads	$100.00
February	Google ads	100.00
March	Google ads, newspaper ad x 4	500.00
April	Google ads	100.00
May	Google ads	100.00
June	Google ads, trade show booth	600.00
July	Google ads	100.00
August	Google ads	100.00
September	Google ads	100.00
October	Google ads	100.00
November	Google ads	100.00
December	Google ads, newspaper ad x 4	500.00
	Total	$2,500.00

Chapter 6

Working with the Pet Community to Promote Your Business

orking with the community around you is not only a good way to gain extra advertising it is also a way to establish your pet business is perceived as a community-minded business. Aligning yourself with nonprofit organizations, shelters, or other like-minded businesses can only help you in the future.

1. Shelters and Rescues

Virtually every city and town in North America has at least one animal shelter or rescue organization operating within its vicinity. Get to know how many there are in your area and what types of animals they help. Many operate as nonprofit groups, so research what they may possibly need in terms of additional services or items and consider holding a fundraiser in their honor. It will bring people to your business and get them talking to others about you.

Some individuals have created secondary animal charities strictly to support local shelters or animal rescues. Operation Blankets of Love, founded by Eileen Smulson, in Southern California, is a nonprofit organization that supports rescues and shelters across America by providing blankets and bedding to animals in need. Similarly, Snuggles Project, a support program for Hugs for Homeless Animals, brings quilters and people who crochet together from around the world to create blankets for shelter animals.

Creating a project or filling a need will not only show your pet business in a good light, it is a way to give something meaningful to those in need and positively impact your community. If your business has products or services that can benefit these organizations, this is a good way to help them without breaking the bank.

Ultimately, in the pet industry, people love their pets and helping animals in need can go a long way to strengthen your business. It will show to people that you really care about animals and are not just about the money.

2. Supporting Nonprofit Organizations and Charities

Nonprofit organizations and charities can include shelters and rescues but can also include support programs for animals in need, such as search and rescue teams, K9 units, animal transportation services, animal disaster relief services, and low-income support services for pets. Ultimately, find the organization or charity that most appeals to you on a personal level or the one that aligns most closely with your business type and offer support to them.

Many pet businesses offer continued, long-term support to the charities and organizations that best fit with their business and personal ethics. Sponsorships and donations are common ways of supporting local charities. Some of the larger franchise pet businesses (e.g., PetSmart) have created their own charities and donate a percentage of sales to help fund their efforts, as well as mandated that each franchise work with local rescues and provide an area for the promotion of adoptions.

In the end, you will feel good doing something good, all the while receiving notoriety, recognition, and more clients.

3. Collaborating with Other Pet-Based Businesses

As mentioned in Chapter 5, section **4.3**, you can enter into the fine art of cross promotions. By offering services or discounts to other pet businesses in your area you take out the nasty feel of competition while reaching the pet community through existing avenues. This has the potential to increase your client or customer base while providing you with free advertising. By offering to hand out another company's business cards, if that business does the same for you, it can easily increase the amount of potential customers you reach in a business day with minimal effort or expense.

Imagine all the other ways you could collaborate with similar businesses. Depending on the type of pet business you are opening it is a good idea to introduce yourself and your business to a reputable veterinarian in your area. You never know when an emergency will occur and some vets require you to be an existing patient/business before they will treat emergency cases.

4. Pet Expos

Pet expos can include everything and anything to do with pets. Most welcome pets attending with their human counterparts. This can be a great way to attract new clientele, as you can target all your clientele — humans and animals — at once. Expos are an interactive and fun way to get your business recognized, and for you to check out what your competitors have to offer as well as give you new ideas and avenues to pursue.

In the US, the Global Pet Expo, Super Pet Expo, and SuperZoo are a few of the largest pet expos in the nation attracting thousands of people each year. You may not have a pet expo close to your community, but if you run a business that is online, the expo may be an avenue to promote yourself throughout North America.

Most expos are organized by a production company or a group of industry associates. They offer other pet businesses the opportunity to purchase a booth or table to promote and sell their products or services to consumers attending the expo. You can usually also hand out coupons for discounts at your store to attract new clients.

It is highly recommended that you attend an expo before you start your own pet business to see various options and to ask questions. Besides being a lot of fun, it is a good way to test the waters in the industry and see, firsthand, what is already being offered to the pet population in your area. Pet expos can be held at a local or national level.

Typically an expo differs from a trade show in that it is consumer based. Vendors assemble at one location and consumers attend to purchase products or attend informational seminars. Also, expos provide a way for customers to price compare products in real time. (See section **5.** for more information on trade shows.)

As expos are person-to-person, you must be outgoing. Engage your clientele as they pass by; a smile or eye contact can go a long way in drawing potential customers to your booth. It also allows for you to get a real-time view of your demographic and to whom your business is appealing.

Many vendors offer free draws or give away gift bags allowing potential clients to try a small sample of a product before buying. If the clients and their pets like what you have, they are likely to come to your business.

Also, promoting a nonprofit or an animal charity you work with at the expo will show the public you really care about animals.

If your surrounding area doesn't already host a pet expo, think about hosting one for potential future business expansion. Events like this take a huge time commitment and extreme organizational skills so be prepared. However, the financial returns can be good and it may position your business as a leader in the industry.

5. Trade Shows

Trade shows are typically only open to those already in the industry. They are a great way to view and test new products as they come on the market, and to view up-and-coming technology. Trades shows provide the opportunity to meet future business colleagues and collaborate on new ideas or needed services and products in the pet industry.

In Canada, the Pet Industry Joint Advisory Council (PIJAC) is the voice of the pet industry. It holds trade shows throughout major cities in Canada at various times of the year. It allows for business owners and employees working within the pet industry to attend one or more shows throughout the year.

Typically all costs associated with attending or being a vendor at a trade show are considered tax write-offs. This can equate to the opportunity to advertise and increase revenues while decreasing your tax bill.

Some trade shows operate on an order-revenue basis. This means that you attend to advertise your pet business products or services, and offer order forms, then get billed based on how much you sold. The first trade show I attended was a PIJAC-sponsored trade show in Calgary, Alberta. There were more than 150 pet-business suppliers and pet-oriented businesses present, but not one of them was actually selling anything. This is a true benefit for those who dislike the high-powered sales pitch and just want to be able to see the product or service.

These types of shows are a good resource for seeking out new suppliers and products and receiving information. Many offer discounts for ordering at a trade show or shortly thereafter as an incentive to would-be purchasers. Trade shows also generate promotional hype for new products in the hopes that the excitement will be carried back with businesses to their customers and translate into sales.

Chapter 7 Hiring Staff and Acquiring Equipment

epending on the type of pet business you are opening, your individual staffing and equipment needs will vary. Some of the initial considerations should be how big your business will be at the start (how much staff and equipment you will require when you open), and what ideas you have for future expansion. You will need to consider what equipment can wait until you get more clients and cash flow as opposed to what equipment you will need when you open.

1. Hiring Help

In the beginning you may decide that you don't need any employees because you can do everything yourself. However, as your business grows you might have to hire part-time employees, and eventually, full-time employees. You might also want to consider hiring temporary or contract employees during your busy times through the year, and working on your own for the rest of the time.

1.1 Hiring part-time or full-time employees

When staffing for a retail, grooming, or daycare business, your needs should be basic. Most of these types of businesses can operate with minimal employees when duties are clearly outlined. Of course you, as the owner, would typically be part of the staff as well. This can be a benefit when you are first starting out because the more you can do yourself, the less money you will spend on staffing costs.

Many pet business owners can attest that after years of running their businesses they still put in 20 to 30 hours a week minimum; even with staff and management in place. If you have no intention of putting a lot of time into your business, stop reading now and apply for a job at your local pet store. Owning your own business will always require dedication. After all, it was your passion and insight that urged you to start a business in the first place. As your company's heart and soul, your presence and direction will always be required.

In the United States, employment laws are fairly similar to those in Canada with regard to full-time and part-time employment standards. Many pet business owners utilize more part-time paid staff to avoid having to pay full-time benefits (e.g., sick days, vacation pay), which saves the business money. Check with your state and federal employment standards to be certain of the regulations in your area.

The US Department of Labor enforces the Fair Labor Standards Act (FLSA), which requires employers to pay no less than the federal minimum wage for each hour worked and time and one-half of the employee's regular rate of pay for hours worked in excess of 40 hours in the week for nonexempt workers.

As an employer in the US, you must withhold from your employees' wages the federal income tax, social security, and Medicare. To figure out the amount you have to withhold, the Internal Revenue Service (IRS) offers sample forms on its website at www.irs.gov/businesses/small (accessed September, 2011).

In Canada, full-time constitutes anyone who works 35 hours or more per week, which entitles the employee to holiday pay and vacation pay. As the employer, you are required to pay all taxes, and government deductions. Contact the Canada Revenue Agency (CRA) for more information about employee taxation.

Keep in mind that with any part-time or full-time employee you are responsible to provide them a safe, clean, and honest work environment and to always follow labor laws. In order to fire an employee, there are procedures you must follow such as verbal and written warnings for infractions or you could face a wrongful dismal lawsuit. Check with your state or province for these types of regulations.

1.1a Employee wages

In the United States, minimum wages for an employee performing basic tasks can range from $5.15 per hour by state. According to the labor laws in Canada, minimum employee wages range from $8.75 to $11 per hour by province. Of course, you should plan to pay more than your province or state's minimum for tasks requiring certain skills or training.

You should set aside at least three months' wages for each employee you intend to hire at the start just in case you have a month or two with low cash flow.

1.2 Accredited staffing: contracted employees

Businesses within the pet-service industry typically require a moderate number of staff, with a focus on the staff members that offer complementary skills and certifications to your pet business. If you are the primary service provider for your pet business, then you may only require one other certified practitioner or assistant.

Staffing can mean having standard paid employees or hiring temporary employees. For example, if you are an animal physiotherapist opening a pet physiotherapy center, you could hire your additional service practitioners such as dog masseuses or animal-homeopathic practitioners as temporary employees.

1.2a Paying temporary employees

A benefit of subcontractors or temporary employees can mean you can be less financially responsible. Subcontracted employees are responsible for their own taxes, income generation, and other government deductions. Using subcontracted employees means you will not be responsible for paying vacation, disability, or statutory holiday pay. Refer to the Internal Revenue Service or Canada Revenue Agency for specific information regarding the regulations for subcontracted employees.

Those working in the pet health-care fields will be skilled, and expect a higher wage. Most professionals are subcontracted, contracted, or on a salary basis. Contracted employees are usually hired at a certain wage or salary for a determined period of time.

Some pet business owners offer signing bonuses or incentives to work for their business. Do your research of what is common in your area and be realistic. Offering too much can leave little room for wage increases in the future or place a strain on your financial resources at the start. Offering too little can cause high turnover, or people not taking the job in the first place. In the end, anything can and will happen so be prepared. Cover all your bases so at the end of the day, no matter what happens, you know you have done everything possible to hire the right people for your business.

1.3 Where to find qualified staff

Once you have determined the type (i.e., subcontracted, salary) and amount of employees that will suit your business best in the beginning, you will need to advertise for the position(s). Classifieds, job search websites, and professional forums are all acceptable ways of seeking employees. Even word of mouth can be beneficial if you have connections to others in the pet industry.

Another way is to ask around at colleges and universities to see if they have internship programs. You can hire students that want experience in the field.

1.4 Interviewing potential candidates

When interviewing potential employees for your pet business, besides reviewing their skill levels and how they would benefit your business, you will want to see how they interact with the animals you work with.

An animal should be present during each interview and the potential candidate's interactions with the animal should be considered part of the interview process. Be alert to the response the animal gives the interviewee. If you notice a normally friendly animal shying away, consider the behavior carefully. Animals will often prevail where our own instincts fail.

For many types of pet businesses, experience is necessary when seeking employment working with and around animals. I have witnessed more injuries for both humans and animals that were caused from inexperience than from anything else. As well, those with experience working with animals or who have pets themselves are more likely to offer their knowledge to potential clients or customers. That's not to say that those who are inexperienced should not receive employment; rather a recommendation that any inexperienced employees are supervised at first to ensure the safest conditions for all those employed by or shopping at your pet business.

Questions to consider asking potential employees during an interview should include but are not limited to their experience, future ambitions, and references for past employment.

2. Buying Equipment and Products

What equipment do you need to start your business? During your first few days of business you may discover that you don't have all the equipment that you need. However, by planning out what an average day at your pet business will look like you can create a list of necessary items you will use and require from day one.

Equipment costs for a retail business can range from $10,000 to $50,000 or more, depending on the type of pet business you wish to create. Basic items would consist of a computer, printer and fax, office supplies, debit card and credit card machine, cash registers, service counter, office furniture, and, of course, any product.

For service-oriented businesses, equipment costs can range from $10,000 to $500,000 or more, again depending on the type of business. Some items in the higher-cost category consist of treadmills, hydrotherapy pools, ultrasounds, medical equipment, and exam tables.

You may be able to buy some used items from Craigslist or Kijiji, which can be inexpensive ways to obtain the necessary equipment. Also check local thrift stores and liquidation outlets for deals on basic items such as office furniture.

Never skimp on important items such as medical or grooming equipment. Lower grade equipment will usually equate to less than adequate results. Imagine opening a vet clinic after purchasing a secondhand orthoscope that always needs the light replaced, or an x-ray machine that was thousands of dollars cheaper than a new one but never takes clear images.

With some used equipment, you may end up paying for repairs or replacements which can cost much more than new equipment. In the worst-case scenario, malfunctioning equipment could cause you to shut down your business until it is fixed. Remember that one unhappy client can, and likely will, tell at least three other people about his or her experience at your pet business, which could cost you potential clients. There is always room for expansion so starting your business with a few high-quality items and waiting for the nonessentials is a better option than cutting costs to have everything at the start.

Research all products and manufacturers for any equipment you want to purchase. Look for suppliers that will offer discounts, and be skeptical if a deal seems too good to be true.

Expensive equipment can cost tens of thousands of dollars so most companies selling these types of products will offer lease-to-own options with a certain percentage down if you have a good credit report.

Depending on the type of pet business you are starting your equipment needs will vary. For example, if you are opening a retail pet store which sells raw food, you will need a freezer to store the food. You will also need storage racks and free-standing displays to showcase products. If you are starting a high-end boutique, you will need to place as much focus on your décor as you would your products. Check out similar pet businesses in your area and see what they are offering and how they are set up.

2.1 Setting up accounts with suppliers

In order to receive products for sale, you will need to find reliable supply companies. Most suppliers require you to be a business owner in the pet industry with a valid business license. Many will ask for your licence number and a credit card to be retained on your file for all future orders. Should these numbers change, it will be up to you to notify any and all suppliers you deal with.

Typically the ways to purchase from suppliers are cash on delivery (COD), prepayments (usually by check), cash, credit card, or invoicing (which may include a percentage set by the supply company, interest penalties, and the need for some form of financial backing such as a credit card). Watch for those suppliers that want to charge a high interest rate because you will usually end up paying a higher price for products received and you may not make much profit, if any.

Be aware of the minimum cost of orders from product suppliers. On average the minimum cost will be at least $150 per order. Some suppliers have been known to set a much higher minimum limit of $1,000 or more. If you are only looking to order a few items, high minimums can be a huge deterrent to using certain suppliers.

Other considerations when choosing suppliers is lead time. Some suppliers operate on demand so if you're a smaller business, you may be stuck waiting for back orders or forced to accept longer delivery waits, which can reduce your customer loyalty. Your customers will not want to wait too long for products.

Chargebacks can alleviate some of this delivery stress by enabling pet business owners to become more specific with their agreements with suppliers. According to www.inventoryops.com (accessed September, 2011), "A chargeback is a financial penalty placed against a supplier by a customer when a shipment to the customer does not meet the agreed-upon terms and conditions. Examples of where suppliers may be charged back would include late shipments, or lack of proper packaging and labeling in some cases (compliance labels)."

Also, know the supplier's return policy before you place an order. Each supplier will have a different method for accepting returns on unused, unneeded items, or damaged products or supplies by you or the supplier. Some suppliers will offer straight-across returns, while others will only offer credit. Remember to always read the fine print on your contract with your suppliers, and on your invoices.

Virtually every supply company offers online catalogs and ordering options so check around. Don't get stuck biting off more than you can chew under the pretense that you have few other choices. Be careful with your orders from the beginning until you get to know your clients and their needs and wants.

2.2 Selling products on consignment

Obtaining products on consignment is one way to have products on hand without paying for them up front or once they have been delivered. Some pet clothing, accessories, and art are sold on a consignment basis.

An agreement is reached between you and the producer regarding the percentage of the item once it has been sold. You and the producer will also come to an agreement about how long the item will be displayed before the producer can take the items back. Payouts are given monthly to the producer for products sold. This allows for you to test your market without losing revenues if the product doesn't sell.

2.3 Tracking your inventory

Regardless of whether you open a retail pet business or a pet-service business, you will need a way to track your inventory. Point-of-Sale (POS) systems not only operate as a computerized till, they track your sales and inventory, and generate purchase orders for suppliers.

Some POS system vendors to consider would be Micros, MultiPost, Toshiba Tec America, PC America, and CRM Software Solutions.

Try to stay clear of outdated DOS POS systems. They are less expensive but they do not offer the capabilities that newer programs do. Old systems can also be more complicated for you and your staff to use.

Chapter 8

Ethical Practices When Working with Animals

Animals have worked alongside humans for centuries. Standing beside man in the fields and in battle, our animal companions have historically been our greatest allies and helpers. Part of giving back to their continued service starts by treating all animals you encounter with dignity and respect.

When you are considering starting a business involving animals it's a good idea to take an objective look at your ideals and perspectives on all animals. Ask yourself the following questions:

🐾 Why do I want to work with animals?

🐾 Are there some animals I favor more than others?

🐾 Am I better qualified to work with one species over another?

🐾 Do I have any phobias related to any kind of animals?

The answer to these questions will give you a good idea as to which direction you should take your business. Those who choose to work with animals seldom do so because it is an easy business venture. When working with or around animals there needs to be a great deal of energy, time, and thought spent on their needs. At its basic level, working with animals requires you to become a bit of an interspecies communicator and educator.

In recent years, the treatment of our four-legged associates by the general population has vastly improved, yet there is still a long way to go in terms of equality for all creatures. As the movement shifts towards animals being regarded more like members of the family, more thought and care is being put into their well-being which I hope translates to the eventual universal good treatment of all animals. Many "pet folk" can attest to their hearts going out to the stray cat in the alley, or feeding the homeless dog down the street because it reminded them of their own beloved pets at home. It is this kind of emotion that generally tends to promote the animal advocate in all of us.

The pet industry is definitely a multifaceted consumer market in that you are catering to two types of clients at all times, both the pets and their owners; hence, any marketing strategies for your business should be aimed at both targets. Regardless of which side of the industry you choose to enter keep in mind that the success of your business will depend on this simple strategy.

Regardless of the various arguments associated with the proper and improper way to treat our pets, especially canines and felines, it is safe to say that there is a definite humanization of our pets that occurs to some extent within today's pet-owner population. As a pet-oriented business owner it is recommended that you become familiar with what humanization means in all aspects.

Any pet service offered, no matter how it is defined, should be designed with each pet's unique individuality and needs in mind. For example, you may have clients that refer to their pets as a member of the family and modify their daily routines to include them as such, including accessing traditionally human-oriented services such as weekly massages or acupuncture. While this increases consumer and business options, thereby expanding the pet industry, our pets are a species altogether different from humans.

That is not to say that you shouldn't cater to the human clientele requesting the service for their pets, just that the service should be clearly defined as a pet service in all aspects and carried out as such. It is not appropriate to open a dog-massage therapy center because you are trained as a human massage therapist and you love dogs. However, if you took the appropriate training in dog massage and dog anatomy, would have a great start for a service-based pet business.

Introduction of new legislation in the United States and Canada has paved the way for great developments in the way animals are treated within our society, to protect the rights of working animals. According to the American Humane Association, the Animal Welfare Act (2007) requires that "minimum standards of care and treatment be provided for certain animals bred for commercial sale, used in research, transported commercially, or exhibited to the public. Individuals who operate facilities in these categories must provide their animals with adequate care and treatment in housing, handling, sanitation, nutrition, water, veterinary care, and protection from extreme weather and temperatures. Although federal requirements established acceptable standards, they are not ideal. Regulated businesses are encouraged to exceed the specified minimum standards" (www.americanhumane.org, accessed June, 2011).

Similarly, Section 2(1) of the *Animal Protection Act* (APA) in Alberta states that "no person shall cause or permit an animal of which he or she is the owner or the person ordinarily in charge to be or to continue to be in distress."

The APA also states that an animal is in distress if it is —

🐾 deprived of adequate shelter, ventilation, space, food, water, veterinary care, or reasonable protection from injurious heat or cold;

🐾 injured, sick, in pain, or suffering; or

🐾 abused and subjected to undue hardship, privation, or neglect.

Not only should you be aware of the definitions of distress when working with or around animals, there must also be due care and attention given to the level of care they are receiving at all times.

These protocols must be followed explicitly. If you are working with animals or providing them with a service as your main business objective, you must take their well-being into consideration, at all times.

There needs to be a strong personal incentive to always treat those animals you work with or for with dignity and respect. The success of your business will only ever be as good as your relationship with the animals you work around. Many potential clients will want to see how you engage their companions before they hire you. Respecting their beloved pets will go a long way to securing future business and client referrals.

1. Be Aware

It is the obligation of anyone working with animals to place the animals' needs first, and to always be aware of the present situation. Situations can change rapidly when working with animals. Their senses are far more refined than those of humans; therefore, they will be aware of any changes far before you will. For example, while I was working in a seniors' residence, providing animal-assisted therapy, the rabbit I was working with, Daisy, suddenly became very agitated. She began to dig frantically with her front paws, at the covers on the bed in which the client was laying, and making honking and snorting noises. I had no idea what prompted this sudden shift in her demeanor. Within a few seconds I found out the cause as the client began to seize while having a stroke. Daisy had preempted the client's physiological change.

While working you need to be hypersensitive to your surroundings. While animals will react to change primarily through instinct it is up to their human counterparts to lend rationality and logic to any given situation. It is also up to you to have the necessary skills, prior to working with any animal, to diffuse stressful situations.

These are a few simple steps to employ prior to starting any job with animals:

- Go into any job with a clear mind when working with or around animals. With today's hectic lifestyles you would be surprised how difficult this can be.

- Focus on the present moment. Accidents can quickly occur if proper attention is not being paid to your surroundings at all times.

- Have fun. All animals, including humans, are extremely attuned to negative energy; some animals far more than others. Always keep a calm, assertive energy around any animal.

2. Ethical Purchasing

Ethical purchasing is the act of supporting companies who have the least impact on the environment and the animal kingdom. Around the world people are making conscious efforts to purchase ethically, and the pet industry is no exception. Natural litters, organic-fabric toys and accessories, holistic food options, and eco-friendly pet products are gaining in popularity.

There is also considerable attention being paid to those companies who do not test their products on animals. Research the values and ethics of pet-supply companies and align yourself with those companies who match your own business's ethics. As the business owner, you will want to be able to stand behind each of your products and services.

3. Ethical Business Practices

Your business practices should reflect your ethics and high standards at all times. Not only does this include customer service, but the way you treat your suppliers and staff as well. Follow the golden rule: "Do unto others as you would have them do unto you."

Have a customer service plan and protocol so that you know exactly how you will handle hypothetical situations before they occur. Maintain a fair return and refund or exchange policy. Clients appreciate knowing that their concerns are taken seriously. When you take steps to ensure they are happy every time they visit your pet business you will promote client loyalty.

Keep in good standing with suppliers and delivery services. They are the lifeblood of your pet business. You will rely on them for all products and supplies so make sure your orders are paid on time, in full. Ensure that good rapport is built from the start.

Treat your staff well. As the face of your business they will reflect your leadership in the way they handle customers. Respect their input and opinions and offer bonuses (cash or other types of incentives) for jobs well done.

Your business can influence many people and pets so keep this in mind. For example, an ethically run doggy daycare can influence others to start the same type of business in the city they live in or prompt others to question doggy daycares that are not doing things so ethically. This can help a significant number of pets that might have been receiving unfair treatment. Never take for granted the life of a pet or another person's furry family member.

Chapter 9

Future Trends of the Pet Industry

You have chosen to enter into one of the fastest developing industries in the world. More and more consumers are seeking out similar or the same products and services for their companion animals as for themselves. As more animals are treated as members of the family, the demand for pet-based products and services will continue to grow.

1. The Growth of the Pet Industry in the Last Decade

In the past decade the pet industry has grown exponentially, doubling in revenue in North America. Today's pet industry presents lucrative business opportunities for many. According to the American Pet Products Association (APPA), the average amount spent on North American pets is $48.35 billion in 2010, and projected revenues for 2011 are expected to be $50.84 billion (www.americanpetproducts.org/press_industrytrends.asp, accessed October, 2011).

The increase is due in large part to pet owners no longer supplying just the basic necessities for their pets; these days there is no end to the products and services one can lavish on their beloved pet. It seems the attitude of the public in regards to their animal companions has changed from the old-fashioned attitude of "It's just a pet" to the new and improved attitude of "What do you mean just a pet? They're family."

According to the 2011 to 2012 APPA National Pet Owners Survey (www.americanpetproducts.org/press_industrytrends.asp, accessed September, 2011), 62 percent of US households own a pet. Approximately 86.4 million of these pets are of the feline persuasion while 78.2 million are canines. These numbers are staggering and offer a great incentive to open a business in this industry. Within the last decade the number of households in the United States whom have one or more pets has increased by 10 percent. In 1988, the first year the APPA survey was conducted, 56 percent of US households owned a pet as compared to 62 percent in 2008.

The United States' pet expenditures have close to doubled from $28.5 billion USD in 2001 to $50.84 billion USD in 2011, with no end in sight for this ever-growing industry. Basic expenditures on pets include items such as the following:

- Food ($19.53 billion USD)

- Supplies and medicine ($11.4 billion USD)

- Vet care ($14.11 billion USD)

- Live animal purchases ($2.15 billion USD)

- Pet services such as grooming and boarding ($3.65 billion USD)

These numbers can help with many components of your business plan. Each household in the United States with pets spends an average of $1,600 USD annually on their pets. These numbers are good news for people wanting to start a pet-related business.

In Canada, as of the printing of this book, 55 percent of households have a dog or cat and 19 percent have a fish, bird, or other small animal. The pet industry in Canada is estimated at $5.8 billion CAD annually with the average annual expenditure per household estimated at $420 CAD (www.statcan.gc.ca, "Table 4-1 Average expenditure per household, Canada, provinces and territories, recent years — Canada" accessed October, 2011).

The pet industry has seen robust growth due to the humanizing or anthropomorphizing of pets (owners treating animals as people) and the continuous seeking of quality products and services for these extended family members.

2. What the Pet Industry Is Today

The sky is the limit if you have a little ingenuity. Virtually anything and everything can be marketed to and for the pet population. Services that used to be just for humans but today can be for pets too are —

- Spa packages

- Massage therapy

- Physiotherapy

- Doggy daycares

- Dog spots

- Psychotherapy

- Canine-personality assessments

Specialty products may include the following:

- Therapeutic bath soaps
- Halloween costumes
- Birthday cards
- Dog clothing
- Animal jewelry
- Holistic products

Future pet businesses that are gaining ground include:

- Physiotherapy centers
- Daycare and exercise centers
- Acupuncture clinics
- Pet-care attendants for the disabled, injured, or seniors

Recently cited as "the modern family" by *Psychology Today* magazine, couples with pets are paving the way for an increase in consumer demand for pet-related products. Pets are considered by many to be furry family members. People take them everywhere, including on vacation. People pamper and spoil their pets, celebrate their birthdays, and even buy them Christmas presents! Many individuals can attest to referring to their pets as furry kids. Many emulate this point of view through their attachment and spending patterns. As long as mainstream society agrees with this perspective, the pet industry will continue to be lucrative.

The product and service options we now have for our companion animals far exceed their necessities. They emulate all the finer points of living we would bestow on ourselves. Pet owners are able to choose grooming packages for their pets that are reminiscent of an upscale spa. Pedicures are offered to a variety of species, complete with nail polish. For those who don't like to travel, mobile grooming facilities have been created to bring the spa to your pet. Even using mouthwash and electric toothbrushes on canines and felines has become routine.

Stress release options similar to those we would choose for ourselves are also made available to the average pet. From yoga, reiki, and massage, to herbal and homeopathic remedies, our companion animals can benefit from various alternative therapies as part of their health regime.

Also, puzzle and game toys are being used to enhance our dogs' memories and other cognitive functions as the study of canine psychology is building in momentum.

There are products specifically designed to make the common duties associated with pet care more convenient. High-tech products including GPS collars, invisible fences, automatic doors, feeders and watering units, digital monitoring, and security systems are assisting families in taking care of their companion animals with less effort and more efficiency than ever before.

Pet owners can even be assisted with cleaning duties by automated, self-cleaning litter boxes; disposable cleaning cloths for canines and felines; vacuums, steam cleaners, and cleaning products specifically designed for pet messes; and natural enzymes and air fresheners formulated to eliminate pet odors. There are even companies who offer backyard cleaning and "poop scooping" services.

Many brand-name human-oriented companies are becoming aware of how mainstream and innovative the pet industry has become and are beginning to compete against traditional pet companies. According to the American Pet Products Association, companies such as Bed Head, Louis Vuitton, Origins, and Ed Hardy all offer lines of pet products under their logos. Their products include everything from pet shampoo, clothing, toys, collars, leashes, and gourmet treats and food.

Also, well-known hotel chains across North America, such as Holiday Inn, Howard Johnson, and Best Western have adopted pet friendly policies or have sectioned off whole floors in their hotels in order to accommodate pets who travel with their families. Some boutique hotels, such as the Palomar, near Beverly Hills, California, take luxury pet accommodation one step further by offering pet beds, treats, complimentary food and water dishes, and a gift bag upon arrival. As well, for pets' convenience, they offer pet sitting, a licensed pet masseuse, and an on-call veterinarian, 24 hours per day.

From monogrammed carriers and personalized luggage to digital collar tags, the majority regard their pets as true members of the family and wish to ensure their companion animals benefit from all the comforts society has to offer.

3. Further Expansion of Your Business

After you have achieved success, you may consider expanding your business. This could include changing your location to accommodate more clients, taking on additional services or products, or joining forces with another business. Another option to consider in the future may be franchising your business. Regardless of what you decide, change can be good.

Do not be afraid to be the first to do something new and innovative. If your business plan is solid, and you have done your research, go for it. Trends are always changing with time so be sure to balance any trend-based pet business with a stable product or service that will always be in demand.

All business plans should include a section with future expansion goals. These should be realistic and attainable within five to ten years of your pet business being in operation. Don't be afraid to modify your ideas. Just because something was written down does not make it ironclad.

Take a look at where the industry stands today. What options are provided? Are there any gaps in services? Is there an existing pet business on which you could greatly improve? These are all questions that will lead you to your perfect and profitable pet business. Look for a need within the industry and plan to fill that need.